EXQUISITE TEARS

Exquisite Tears

Messengers Straight from Your Heart

DIANN COCKERHAM

Exquisite Tears: Messengers Straight From Your Heart

Copyright © 2021 by Diann Cockerham

Hardcover ISBN: 9780578960531

Paperback ISBN: 9798542568782

The author has tried to recreate events, locales, and conversations from her memory and research into emotions and tears. In order to maintain anonymity, in some instances the author may have changed the names of individuals and places. The author may have changed some identifying characteristics and details such as physical properties, occupations, and places of residence.

All Scripture quotations, unless otherwise indicated, are taken from the Holy Bible, New International Version®, NIV®. Copyright ©1973, 1978, 1984, 2011 by Biblica, Inc.™ Used by permission of Zondervan. All rights reserved worldwide. www.zondervan.com. The "NIV" and "New International Version" are trademarks registered in the United States Patent and Trademark Office by Biblica, Inc.™

Scripture quotations marked KJV are taken from the KING JAMES VERSION (KJV): KING JAMES VERSION, public domain.

Scripture quotations marked ESV are from The ESV® Bible (The Holy Bible, English Standard Version®), copyright © 2001 by Crossway, a publishing ministry of Good News Publishers. Used by permission. All rights reserved.

Cover and interior design by Adam Thomas

Cover image by Joyce McCown (via Unsplash.com)

Contents

To the loving memory of my brother
Calvin Gordon Crone
And to the Holy Spirit, my best friend and faithful inspiration
With deep devotion and gratitude

Introduction

The eyes have one language everywhere.
—George Herbert

I have always, even as a little girl, wondered what I was supposed to be. My teachers and friends would ask me what I wanted to be when I grew up and with each question came a different answer. When I learned about dreams and making them come true, I tried to decide what would make me happy as a grown-up so that I could dream about it and make it come true. I had a hard time deciding and changed my mind daily. My parents would try to help by pointing out all the ways I was special and all the things I did well. Mother said I should be a teacher because I did such a good job taking care of little sisters and kids in the neighborhood. Daddy said I should use my imagination because I always played make-believe and loved creating a new song or a new something to do every day.

They both said that with whatever I did when I grew up, it would be important that I learn not to cry so much.

That's right—I've always had a unique connection with emotions and tears. There are many reasons why. One of them is that I have not been able to control my tears through the years. The truth is that tears actually control me in many

1

ways and have a special place in my heart. Tears have come with almost every important event in my life and even some not-so-important ones. I have also experienced a deeply emotional phase when tears just would *not* come for me. This was difficult to understand, and with all of this came a fascination with emotions and feelings, along with the eyes and tears that tell the story. Perhaps this sounds familiar, or maybe you have had a different experience with tears. Tears may not come easily for you or not at all. And yet, however unique we are as humans, tears are as much a part of who we are as anything, and I have learned that they have a special purpose.

Back when I was a curly-haired, five-year-old tomboy, I adored my daddy. All that he said and all that he taught me was absolutely golden. He was an optician who crafted and sold eyeglasses for a living and he was extremely creative, a true artist in many ways. Along with his beautiful singing voice and drawing skills, one of his magical gifts was his talent for creating hand-painted, artificial eyes for people who had lost an eye.

In those days right after World War II, there was a special need for these artificial eyes. Daddy's creations were beautiful and so realistic. He took hours and hours to painstakingly craft each precious eye to perfectly match its mate—the other eye now giving "sight" all alone. They were made of special plastics and after measurements were taken, as with pottery or porcelain, they were baked in plaster molds. Those exquisite works of art would sit right up there on our mantel while they cured in the molds waiting for the finishing touches that would result in a precise fit. I can see them now.

We were never allowed to touch them, but those beautiful, delicate eyes were captivating and came to life when they seemed to wink at us in the flickering firelight. While my sisters and I looked up at them, Daddy would tell us stories of the brave soldiers and how they lost their sight fighting for our freedom. He would explain how the magic of tears made it possible for the new artificial eye to move. Although it would never see or shed tears of its own, it would fit right in as a partner to the unharmed eye. My sisters and I loved his stories, and our imaginations took us away to the battlefields and bedsides and made us so proud of Daddy and what he was able to do for those brave men.

That is one reason I chose to write a book to explore and share with you the nature and spiritual characteristics of tears. A far more important reason, however, is that I believe God has given us tears as valuable clues and hallmarks of emotion. Imagine the first man and woman communicating and expressing their feelings using words, body language, touching, singing, and dancing—all the wonderful ways of expression that we embrace without even thinking what they might tell us about ourselves. Right up there with these means of expression are tears. What do they tell us about ourselves?

Science tells us that humans, who I believe were made from the beginning in the image of God, are the only creatures known to shed emotional tears. Our tears reveal a powerful connection between thoughts and emotions. I genuinely believe that science and Christianity go hand in hand and that science is the study of God's creation. With that in mind, this book is about exploring together with our hearts and our minds the phenomenal gift of tears and their role in guiding our lives.

I have an academic relationship with emotions through my 2011 dissertation, *Exploring Students' Emotional Experience Within the Distance Learning Environment.*[1] This involved several years of research and looked at how college students felt about and dealt with their exposure to online learning, which was back then a very new educational platform. One of the most interesting outcomes of my study was the documented evidence that when students shared their feelings along with opinions and experiences in their online classes, it enhanced the students' social presence and they better connected to their lessons. Importantly, the study further substantiated the connection between thought and emotions by revealing that these lessons that connected were the ones students remembered and applied along life's journey. I began to see the evidence that emotions guide us on our path through life.

Do you connect tears with emotions? Do tears play an important part in your life? They certainly do for me. The most important times of my life have been punctuated by, heralded by, and proclaimed by tears. It is as if God gives us tears as a sign or a hint that signals *this is important, take note, pay attention.* Mark Batterson, the lead pastor of National Community Church and a best-selling author of more than a dozen books, may have said it best when he suggested that our tears give us clues that guide us to connecting with God's unique desires for our lives.[2]

Our eyes say so much without uttering a word, but the tears they shed take the place of words and tell us so many different things. Each individual in any given circumstance can laugh until they cry, weep softly, or sob with steadily flowing tears that lead to deep anguish. Such extremes! So many varied feelings and emotions come forward through tears that transform eyes. Tears that gild lovely eyes, sad eyes, dark eyes, or bright eyes all serve to evoke messages that only the eyes can convey.

With an ever-changing mix of emotions, for each distinct soul, every tear is unique. Who could ever name them? Some say they are like raindrops, snowflakes, or stars—exquisite treasures never to be numbered, except perhaps by God. The Psalmist wrote, "Record my misery; list my tears on your scroll—are they not in your record?" (Psalm 56:8).

Through the years, my quest for knowing who I should be and what purpose God had in mind for me grew more and more frustrating. What was my destiny? I studied the spiritual gifts and knew mine. I continued to seek more education and pursue more degrees in hopes that along the way I would have that aha! moment and find my destiny. On and on it went, until one day I put it all together. That is what I want to share with you.

Eyes and their tears are important to me and my love affair with them has never faded. It's now come full circle to blend with my longing to know God's plan for me and my enthusiasm for investigating emotions. This book is about exploring every aspect of how we express our emotions with tears and how we learn to discover our destiny.

ONE

Crying is Good for You

The cure for anything is saltwater—sweat, tears, or the sea.

—Isak Dinesen

Have you had the experience of being around someone whom you felt deep in your soul *should* be crying, even crying their eyes out, but who was subdued, quiet, and staring into space? I have been there with a friend in a private place when I felt the uneasiness, the sense of helplessness, and the intuitive knowing that the absence of tears was not only unhealthy but unnatural. I have also personally experienced *invisible tears* and know the adverse effects when tears fail to appear. Certainly, many people do not cry easily, especially when in public, and yet I have experienced the power of tears—real tears—and I know that one tear can be such a precious gift. When the tear refuses to offer its solace, it's as if a switch has been turned off.

Dr. Judith Orloff maintains that it is healthy to cry. In her book *Emotional Freedom*, she discusses the numerous health benefits of tears. Made of saltwater, tears not only remove irritants and lubricate eyes, they also reduce stress hormones and fight pathogenic microbes with antibodies. She explains that our bodies produce three kinds of tears: reflex, continuous, and emotional tears. Each kind plays a different healing role.[1]

Reflex tears allow your eyes to clear out noxious particles when they're irritated by smoke or exhaust. Continuous/basal tears are produced regularly to keep your eyes lubricated. These contain a chemical called "lysozyme," which functions as an anti-bacterial and protects your eyes from infection.

It's the third type, psychic/emotional tears, that have special health benefits. Biochemist and "tear expert" Dr. William Frey of the Ramsey Medical Center in Minneapolis discovered that, unlike reflex tears that are 98 percent water, emotional tears also contain stress hormones that the body excretes through crying. After studying the composition of tears, Frey found that emotional tears shed these hormones and other toxins that accumulate during stress. Additional studies suggest that crying and oxytocin, the "feel-good" hormone, go together. Typically, after crying, your breathing slows, your heart rate decreases, and you enter a calmer biological and emotional state.[2]

Orloff has been enthusiastic about crying for years and says it helps to emotionally clear sadness and stress. She recalls her psychiatric residency at UCLA, when her supervisors watched videos of her with patients and pointed out that she smiled when a patient cried. They said it was inappropriate, but Orloff wholeheartedly disagreed then and still does. She wasn't smiling because her patients were depressed or grieving, she says, but because they were *courageously* healing depression or other difficult emotions with tears. She was happy for their breakthrough.[3]

In thinking back to my friend who could not cry, I know I was sensing the deep need for her to have a breakthrough—for the rallied courage to just fall apart and give in to the awful anguish. To give in with tears. Like the relief that rain brings after a rumbling storm has been brewing, tears bring that release, that peace … and we can finally rest.

I can relate to this. What a relief when I just let go and feel the magical serenity that comes with surrendering to my emotions. Whether I'm feeling anger, happiness, or sadness, the reprieve given by tears is "out of this world." It is much like surrendering to God and His transforming love.

Emotional crying remains one of the human body's more confounding mysteries. Though some other species shed tears reflexively (a result of pain or irritation), remarkably, humans are the only creatures known to shed emotional tears, ones triggered by their feelings. God made man in His image, and we are separated from other creatures in that we have emotions—deeper feelings that reveal a soul or spirit within us and connect us to the Almighty. Throughout the book of Genesis, we find evidence of God's emotions. My favorite reference is found in the first chapter of the Bible: "God saw all that he had made, and it was very good" (Genesis 1:31). When I imagine feeling that way about anything that I have ever created, like my two wonderful sons, it stirs my heart and creates such an intimate connection to my Creator. After all, my finest creations have actually been His handiwork.

Tears are so mysterious that, like dreams, we are still searching for understanding. Modern crying research is in its infancy. However, the recent evidence that they are far more important than scientists once believed pushes Ad Vinger-hoets, a professor at Tilburg University in the Netherlands and the world's foremost expert on crying, to continue his quest for answers. Vingerhoets maintains that tears connect us to one another and are significantly relevant for human nature. Though Charles Darwin once famously said emotional tears were "purposeless," Vingerhoets confidently asserts that Darwin was completely wrong. His research has convinced him that people cry because they need each other.[4]

We do need other people, and we most certainly need health. For certain, we need a heart that keeps on beating. Tears are a human thing and they most often come from the heart, not just the head. Together, we all need to get out of our heads more and into our feelings—with healthy "heartfelt emotions."

TWO

Salt of the Earth

There must be something strangely sacred in salt.
It is in our tears and in the sea.
—Khalil Gibran

Did you know that salt is found in every cell in our bodies? In an adult human, that amounts to about 250 grams, or a cupful. No wonder our tears and sweat are salty. Salt is essential to our ability to function properly. It helps keep the balance of our bodily fluids that carry nutrients and oxygen to every cell. The three types of human tears (reflex, physic/emotional, and continuous/basal) all contain potassium and sodium, two of the most important electrolytes in our bodies. Electrolytes are natural salts that our bodies require for nervous system function. These "salts" transfer information between different nerve cells.

Like our bodies, God created the "bodies of water" that we know and love with salt as a primary component. The National Ocean Service explains that the saltiness of the ocean is the result of several natural influences and processes. Water entering the ocean from rivers is just one of these factors. Rivers and streams flowing in the United States alone discharge an estimated 225 million tons of dissolved solids and 513 million tons of suspended sediment annually to oceans. Throughout the world, rivers carry an estimated four billion tons of dissolved salts to the oceans each year.[1]

On the other hand, scientists maintain that rainwater contains only a slight trace of salt. When evaporation occurs, water is converted to a gaseous state, while the salt is not affected. Since rain is the condensation of that evaporated water, rainwater is pure and not saltwater. However, as my grandkids have noticed, rain sometimes tastes slightly salty because during precipitation, raindrops collect dust particles that contain traces of salt. In other words, rainwater is not salty when it comes out of the cloud because only fresh water went up into the air.[2] Thus, only fresh water comes back out of the cloud. In a nutshell, that's why rivers and streams contain fresh water while the sea is salty. I love explaining this to my grandkids and I seize the moment to make sure they hear the whole story of Jesus asking His followers to be "the salt of the earth" (Matthew 5:13).

All of this speaks to the wonders and the interconnections of God's creations—how they reveal His identity. These scientific explanations and the intricate details of how the oceans and rivers combine to provide for the needs of our world point to divine similarities in much of God's handiwork. We see this divine interconnection in the greatest creation of all—the human body that God created in His own image. We read in Genesis that "the LORD God formed man of the dust of the ground and breathed into his nostrils the breath of life; and the man became a living being" (Genesis 2:7). As with His creation of bodies of water, God used "the salt of the earth" to create the human body, the one in which Jesus Christ ultimately lived and died.

Salt was a necessity of life for Hebrew society during the Old Testament and New Testament periods. The mineral has been used since ancient times in many cultures as a seasoning, a preservative, a disinfectant, a component of ceremonial offerings, and even as a unit of exchange. In Roman times, salt was so precious that it provided a way to pay soldiers. Our English word "salary" comes from the word *salarium,* a name given to the mineral when it functioned as currency. Its value as a rare commodity earned salt the nickname "white gold" during the Middle Ages.[3]

The Bible contains numerous references to salt, and each time we see God's hand and the connectedness. The most notable example is the story I tell my grandkids about when Jesus, during his famous Sermon on the Mount, stated that believers were the "salt of the earth" and warned that it was possible for them to lose their flavor. If believers lost their "flavor," they would be of no benefit to others. They would then only be worthy of being "thrown out and trampled upon by men" (Matthew 5:13).

Jesus tells those wishing to follow him that they must make a difference in the world. The difference made is "the flavor," or good works, sprinkled like salt, which believers are to complete. Making a difference, however, includes even more than actions. According to Paul the Apostle, we must also use our words like salt to season or benefit those we talk with. He wrote, "Be wise in the way you act toward outsiders; make the most of every opportunity. Let your conversation be always full of grace, seasoned with salt, so that you may know how to answer everyone" (Colossians 4:5–6).

Like so many little girls, one of my favorite pastimes was to play "house" with my sisters and the other girls in the neighborhood. Pretending to be like our mothers meant that an important part of our game was preparing and serving a meal to everyone in the family. It began with deciding who was the mother, the daddy, the sister, the brother, and so on. After that, we gathered the ingredients for our "dinner." It was such fun to see what everyone came up with and then to put it all together for cooking, before setting the table and sitting in a circle for "eating" together. The main dish was always a combination of dirt and water. Sometimes we would throw in some sand, but usually we dined on mud pies.

If you have never eaten mud, you need to know that it is salty. In fact, if you compared it to the taste of your tears, you would be amazed at the similarity. Now, mud pies are rather yucky, but that's primarily because of their color and gritty texture, along with the idea of swallowing the ugly, dirty ground we walk on. All in all, though, we stomached a few small bites of those mud pies because of the lovely little toppings: flowers, berries, sprigs of grass, and even some leftover Halloween candy if that was available.

When I think about Jesus teaching his followers to be the salt of the earth, I remember those salty mud pies and clearly understand why humans have salty tears and sweat. It's the best part of my story for the grandkids, that God made us from the earth—the dust, the dirt, and the mud. No wonder we're salty.

After we leave this earth and ascend to heaven, what happens to our salty selves? If there actually are tears in heaven and we weep with the angels, will our spirits be the salt of heaven? Billy Graham said that in heaven we will not be disembodied spirits floating around without any physical form or substance. He pointed out that the Bible tells us something different, that we will be given new bodies when God's plan is complete—bodies created in the image of Christ's body after His resurrection.[4]

A Sacred Pinch of Salt

We know that of the salty earth we are divinely made.
And like the waters of the earth – the rivers, the lakes, the oceans –
Up to heaven we rise.
From there we all emerge – the seas as rain and we as spirit.
Each with a tiny trace of salt. Just a pinch to remind us He is here.
—**D. Cockerham**[5]

THREE

God Collects Our Tears

*Thou tellest my wanderings: put thou my tears
into thy bottle: are they not in thy book?*
—**Psalm 56:8 (KJV)**

As I have grown in understanding of my Creator and developed a relationship that brings daily awareness of His presence, I have come to accept His abiding love. In many ways, it reminds me of my love for my children. I am so thankful to have experienced a mother's precious love, and it does help me better understand God's divine, unconditional love for His beloved children. Still, to go so much further in helping us comprehend God's love, Luke 12:7 tells us that "even the very hairs of your head are numbered." Yes, our loving Father God has numbered each hair on our heads and, as if that isn't enough, He keeps track of and collects our tears (Psalm 56:8).

It is so comforting to know that God collects my tears. When I think of all the years and all the many tears, it is mind-boggling that He would care so much for me. I counted my boys' fingers and toes again and again when they were tiny. As they grew, I counted each bruise and scratch—every single boo-boo was counted and got a special kiss from Mom. I collected and still have locks of their hair and their first baby teeth, but I get misty just thinking how much more loving and caring my Heavenly Father must be to count every single intimate detail of my life.

When I consider my tears, which have been present through all the ups and downs of my life, I am humbled by Psalm 56:8. It reminds me that God is intimately concerned with every aspect of my life—even my tears. To imagine God collecting my tears in a bottle is just so amazing. Really, how very personal! The tears I wept over my first lost love—in His bottle. The time I cried over the fender bender with my brand-new car—in His bottle. Not only does He know us intimately … our every hair, our every breath … but He knows our every tear and collects them and records them in His book. He values them, loves them, understands them, and does not want to misplace them.

I have never found anything hidden away or collected in a bottle. However, I imagine it must be a special feeling to find a bottle and know that someone carefully slipped something inside for someone else to find, either by throwing the bottle out to sea or by carefully hiding it behind a wall. I once watched a television show about a couple who renovated homes. One day, they knocked down a wall and found a Coke bottle atop an inside support crossbeam. It held neither money, nor a confession to a heinous murder, nor a love letter. Inside was simply a note with the hider's name and his confession that he put the bottle there for fun just to see if anyone would one day find it and call him with the discovery. Do you suppose there was more to it than that, perhaps a need to connect or to be remembered, if only by an unknown finder of his bottle? The couple called him. Though it was a bit of a letdown that there wasn't something more exciting inside the bottle, they connected and had fun with the whole thing.

It's in our nature, perhaps, to collect things in bottles as remembrances. Humans have been collecting tears in bottles since ancient times. David remarks on the tear bottle in Psalm 56, as the custom in Biblical times was to collect tears of devotion. The tear bottles had great significance, so much so that when a person was buried, mourners buried the tear bottle with the deceased. The ancients believed that any tears shed for a spiritual cause would be rewarded by God. Thus, tear bottles were very precious to them. If one faced danger and had to flee, tear bottles were saved first.

Early Western cultures, both pagan and Christian, record a long tradition of tear bottles, which are also sometimes called lachrymatory bottles, tear catchers, tear vials, unguentaria, or unguentarium.[1] Professor Ad Vingerhoets, an expert on the study of tears, says that tear bottles have been found in ancient Egyptian, Greek, and Roman societies. Rather than containing actual tears, however, Vingerhoets says it is more likely that the bottles contained ritual oils and perfumes. His research has confirmed that tear bottles were used by sailors and soldiers when they were separated from their loved ones, and, during the nineteenth century, by people who collected their own tears as they mourned the loss of their loved ones.[2]

During the U.S. Civil War, women cried into tear bottles and saved them until their husbands returned from battle. Their collected tears would show the men how much they were adored and missed. Historical references also indicate that tears were saved as a remembrance of loved ones or to pass along to future generations. This is such a tender image of emotions associated with tears: devotion, love, and remembrance.

Recently, I enjoyed listening to the audio book *Ireland*, by Frank Delaney.[3] Set in the Victorian Period of the nineteenth century, the book tells the story of a woman who becomes a widow early in life. She says that she will grieve for one year and one day, which was the custom, and collect her tears in a cup during that time ... then she will pour the tears over her departed husband's gravestone at the end of that time. Once all the moisture was gone from the tear bottle or the cup, it indicated that the time of mourning was at an end. As with our God, the collection of tears was all about devotion, love, and remembrance.[44]

We may think that tears, like water, evaporate. But we know all things are possible with God, and if He is collecting our tears—saving them and cherishing them—they do not evaporate. They do not roll down our cheeks and vanish forever. No, they go into His bottle. It is such an intriguing but profound image to affirm that with our Lord and Savior, everything about us is precious, especially our tears.

With God who keeps track of all our emotions, His devotion, love, and remembrance of our tears never ends.

FOUR

Love and Tears:
A Powerful Combination

*And now these three remain: faith, hope and
love. But the greatest of these is love.*
—Corinthians 13:13

As little people, we know the power of tears. What is more powerful than a human baby's cries? Babies lack physical strength and language at first, and it takes a while before they learn to turn over, let alone crawl or run away. Not much power there. No, the real power God gave the tiny baby is the ability to cry, and he instilled love in those who respond to the crying because they have the deep joy and daunting responsibility of caring for that tiny soul. What a powerful combination: love and tears.

A baby cries to communicate. Infants have no words, just gurgles and bubbles, but crying says it all for them. From "I am miserable and need my diaper changed," to "I am sleepy and hungry," a baby's messages can be conveyed through crying and tears. Yes, we learn about crying early and we don't need instruction. When the helpers who take care of us react, we instinctively learn the importance of tears and can vary their intensity to communicate our needs by the time we are only a few days old. This is such an awesome gift from the very start. It's our first communication tool.

Tears don't only get us attention when we are little. They go right on helping us get through life in many special, sometimes intriguing, ways. As we grow from being babies, we learn that tears communicate far more than just our basic needs. They begin to communicate our emotions. They hold power and, above all, remind us that we are made in God's image.

Women cry. That's something of a foregone conclusion, but what a blessing. Studies have found that women cry an average of 3.5 times a month, almost twice as much as men. This is quite a difference and, although the tears do get men's attention, they are often uncomfortable with crying. This difference is readily apparent when watching new parents adjust to life with an infant. Not only does a man feel a little awkward holding the baby, changing diapers, and doing feedings, but he usually gets super anxious when the baby cries. Meanwhile, the new mother has had much more experience with crying (twice as much as her husband) and adapts more easily to being awakened in the middle of the night several times. Don't get me wrong—new dads come around. One of my favorite memories was watching both of my sons cuddle their new babies as they walked them around the house, up and down the hallway, for as long as it took to lull them back to sleep. What we see in those moments is the power of tears and love coming together to build a relationship that will last a lifetime.

Yes, women have the good fortune of being friendly with

tears. While God, no doubt, thinks women deserve the gift of tears or need these attention-getters, the truth is, women probably are so busy doing and being everything for everyone else that God uses them to get *our* attention. He absolutely does this with one most memorable sound, the sound every mother waits nine months to hear—*crying*. Each mother clearly remembers the delightful sound of her baby's first cry. If you are a mother, you are probably just like me and get misty when you remember the first time you heard your child's wail, saw that face and those eyes, that fabulous little wrinkled face … tears and all! What a glorious memory. Crying for a woman becomes a complex part of life that embodies all that God has to offer.

Men certainly cry as well, but as best I can tell, they never do get good at dealing with tears. When I was little, my daddy would melt when any of his five children *tuned up*, as he would say, and tears pooled on our eyelashes. That was all it took. He was very willing to give my brother or any of us girls a hug, wipe away our tears, and, of course, kiss and make it better. Is being more familiar with tears a God-given advantage for women? Possibly, and heaven knows, we often need it. While tears may not be exclusive gifts for women, they do seem to get attention, and our tears certainly help us understand when someone else needs attention. This lovely Scottish poem by an unknown author says so much about the powerful combination of love and tears.

Why God Gave Women Tears
A little boy asked his mother
"Why are you crying?"
"Because I'm a woman,"
she told him.
"I don't understand,"
he said.
His mum just hugged him
and said, "And you never
will."
Later the little boy asked
his father, "Why does mother seem to cry for
no reason?"
"All women cry for no reason," was all his dad could say.
The little boy grew up and became a man,
still wondering why women cry.
Finally he put in a call to God; and when God got on
the phone, he asked, "God, why do women cry so
easily?"
God said:
"When I made the woman she had to be special.
I made her shoulders strong enough to carry the weight of the
world; yet, gentle enough to give comfort
I gave her an inner strength to endure childbirth and
the rejection that many times comes from her children.
I gave her a hardness that allows her to keep going
when everyone else gives up, and take care of her

family through sickness and fatigue without
complaining. I gave her the sensitivity to love her children under
any and all circumstances, even when her child has
hurt her very badly.
I gave her strength to carry her man through his
faults and fashioned her from his rib to protect his
heart. I gave her wisdom to know that a good man never
hurts his woman, but sometimes tests her strengths and
her resolve to stand beside him unfalteringly.
And finally, I gave her a tear to shed
This is hers exclusively to use whenever it is
needed.
You see:
The beauty of a woman is not in the clothes she wears,
the figure that she carries, or the way she combs her
hair. The beauty of a woman must be seen in her eyes,
because that is the doorway to her heart—the place
where love resides."[1]

———————

The power and wonder of tears are perhaps best understood when reading the three passages in the Bible where we
are told that our Lord and Savior Jesus Christ felt emotion and
wept. The shortest verse in the King James Version, "Jesus wept"
(John 11:35), records when Jesus felt the piercing pain of grief
and asked where His friend Lazarus's body was buried. Next,
Jesus wept passionately with sadness over Jerusalem's choice to
reject Him (Luke 19:41). The third recorded time Jesus wept
was in the garden of Gethsemane, the night before His cruci-

fixion, when he felt sorrow and great distress (Hebrews 5:7).

As we discover in reading about Jesus, tears express emotions and are a magnificent part of life as a human being made in God's image. When He created humans in Eden, God intended for us to use tears as a lifelong way to connect with one another. For infants, crying is the only way to communicate, but God did not intend for people to forsake tears as they grow and become adults. With every highlight and even the lowlights, crying serves throughout our lives as a way to express our feelings and emotions. As the Scottish poem reminds us, just looking into someone's eyes takes us to their heart, where God planted his seed of love when they were first created. That love needs to be nurtured by the moistness of our tears, the richness of a life well-lived, and the presence of the Holy Spirit caring for God's beloved garden of our heart.

FIVE

When Men Cry

If you laugh, you think, and you cry, that's a full day. That's a heck of a day. You do that seven days a week, you're going to have something special.
—Jim Valvano

Until recently, many cultures believed that tears were a sign of manliness. World history and literature are filled with males who cried publicly. A man's tears meant that he lived by a code of values and was concerned enough to show emotion when things went badly. Medieval warriors and Japanese samurai cried during times of epic tragedy.[1] In the Anglo-Saxon poem *Beowulf*, when Beowulf was killed by a dragon, his warriors were "disconsolate—and wailed aloud for their Lord's decease."[2] In early Western culture, a man's capacity to cry indicated his honesty and integrity. Abraham Lincoln shed tears during his speeches when he believed that sharing emotions was appropriate.[3]

But from the eighteenth to twentieth centuries, the population became increasingly urbanized, and changes in the economy required men and women to work together in factories and offices where emotional expression and even private conversations were discouraged. As Tom Lutz explains in *Crying: The Natural and Cultural History of Tears*, there was a great deal of concern about emotions interfering with the smooth running of things.[4]

Fast forward to more recent history, and we find that men shedding tears is often regarded as less than masculine. The explanation may well be that men have been taught, point-by-point, not to feel, not to cry, and not to find words to express any emotion. They're instructed to "man up" because "big boys don't cry." Boys are conditioned to fear being called a "sissy," and often men never lose that fear.

The truth is that our culture has grown to value a certain kind of boy—those who are ambitious and popular, those who can make anyone laugh, and those who won't back down from insults or mean words. Being ambitious, popular, funny, or assertive isn't a problem, but hiding other aspects of being a human boy, in the name of "manning up," can become problematic. As a result, Daphne Rose Kingma, author of *The Men We Never Knew*, has said we've given up on men by deeming them the gender without feelings. Boys are socialized in a way that diminishes their ability to deal with emotions.[5]

Though men may not be comfortable communicating their feelings, they still feel and feel intensely. Many times, men may convert one feeling into another. Feelings that they may consider "feminine," such as sadness or helplessness, may be converted into feelings like anger or pride—feelings that are more socially acceptable for men to display. Men may express emotions only in places where they feel safe and when the expression of feelings is considered acceptable. Just look at how men act when it comes to sports.[6] For example, my husband, who played football throughout high school and college, will openly tear up during a game when his team wins or when a player gets seriously injured. And when he's sharing details with family or close friends—sometimes every single detail—of the last unforgettable minutes of a critical game from years ago, his feelings are on full display. It is not uncommon to see men at sporting events express great excitement and affection, giving each other hugs and high-fives. Even football and hockey players, considered to be the ultimate examples of "manly" men, seem relaxed expressing their feelings with each other during a game. Where else would you see men slapping each other playfully on the fanny? Put these same men in another setting, and you probably won't see the same level of warmth, honesty, and emotion.

In his 2016 article for *The Charlotte Observer*, "Did Luke Kuechly Make it Safe for a Man to Cry?", Théoden Janes discussed a bit of the conundrum we all face about grown men crying.[7] His commentary was accompanied by a large, color photo of Carolina Panthers middle linebacker Luke Kuechly in tears after being injured while playing the New Orleans Saints. Thursday Night Football also ran shots of Kuechly with tears streaming down his face, so viewers all over the country had a chance to weigh in on how they felt about his tears. Sympathetic people flooded social media with comments. Of course, Kuechly was something of a rarity in the NFL—hugely popular among fans across broad demographics and widely respected around the NFL by other players. On top of that, he wasn't crying over a tough loss or after getting into a fight with an opponent. As Janes said, Kuechly was badly hurt and quite possibly overcome with emotion at the prospect of his season ending prematurely. Lest we think the entire world of sports had turned a new leaf, Janes went on to share that despite the flood of sympathetic responses on social media, an unscientific Twitter poll showed that 30 percent of seventy-two respondents voted Kuechly "a wimp." How many men? How many women? No breakdown was given.

Janes candidly shared his own personal experience with crying, triggered by the painful realization that his daughter was growing up too quickly. He pondered whether that qualified as a good reason for a grown man to cry but asserted that he honestly did not care. His closing undoubtedly left many readers agreeing that they would like to think Luke Kuechly felt the same way.[8]

Perhaps, after decades of berating men for their tears, people may be returning to the idea that crying is a male strength. A generation ago, the tears of England's first crying footballer, Gazza (Paul Gascoigne), created a media sensation. Today, footballers' tears go almost unnoticed, and it's a similar story in other sports. Pictures of Andy Murray, Novak Djokovic, or Roger Federer shedding tears at a Wimbledon final no longer attract surprise or disapproval. In the United States, pro golfer Dustin Johnson cried tears of elation after winning the 2020 Masters Tournament. Earlier that year, Michael Jordan and other famous athletes cried openly at the funeral of their friend, basketball legend Kobe Bryant, bringing tears to unembarrassed viewers' eyes.

As cultural norms shift back toward acceptance of the

emotional man, will we all adjust our personal perspectives around the idea? This change may be slow in coming. After all, many men maintain that raising a strong boy means discouraging tears, and others seem to doubt whether women genuinely want to see male vulnerability on display. As with most behaviors, a man crying is considered more appropriate in some situations, such as at funerals and when holding his newborn baby, than in others. Whatever our viewpoint, I believe the real task is not only to show good judgment but to refrain from criticizing men simply for shedding tears. They are human, after all.

Isn't it interesting to consider for a moment the situations we just mentioned, when most people think it is acceptable for men to cry? Funerals and new life mark some of the more spiritual moments of a man's life. I love that when it comes right down to it, most people acknowledge the profound truth about the connection between our spirits and emotions for both men and women. The Bible tells us that sharing our feelings with others is helpful in managing emotions and that the Christian life is not meant to be lived alone. God has given us the gift of other believers who can share our emotions. "Rejoice with those who rejoice, weep with those who weep" (Romans 12:15).

As the mother of two boys, I did my best to ensure that my sons grew up to be well-adjusted men who would be comfortable with who they were and with their emotions. I even urged my boys when they were little to talk about their feelings and to share what was going on in their lives. They did resist at times, but I think they understood the importance of having parents who didn't tell them not to cry or that toughness was the only thing that mattered. On the other hand, many boys grow up suppressing their feelings and living a masculine ideal that may put too much pressure on them to be someone else. I believe that we need to be doing more to raise our sons to be emotionally open and empathetic because we value their happiness the same way we do our daughters'.

I especially like the way UN Women Goodwill Ambassador Emma Watson put it in her speech at a special event for the HeForShe campaign, when she asserted that both men and women should feel free to be sensitive and free to be strong because it is time that we all perceive gender on a spectrum and not as two opposing sets of ideas.[9]

SIX
Emotional Intelligence

Let's not forget that the little emotions are the great captains of our lives and we obey them without realizing it.
—**Vincent van Gogh**

Where do our emotions come from? Some say our hearts, while others believe they originate in our souls. No matter how many emotions we have, each one is a function of the amygdalae, the almond-shaped clusters of nuclei located within the temporal lobe of the brain. This is often called *the seat of emotion,* and it is a facet of God's image. Paying attention to our emotions is paying attention to God's voice. Whether it's the voice of sadness, anger, or happiness, we should never ignore how we feel. God is speaking to each of us—as well as to our children.

Perhaps of all the emotions experienced by humans, sadness is usually associated with tears. The basic emotion of sadness occurs for many disparate reasons. For example, we can feel sadness at the loss of a pet, the bombing of the Twin Towers, the death of our grandmother, or even the blame we may feel for complicated cultural struggles that trouble our souls.

31

However basic sadness may be, the tendency is to treat boys and girls differently when it comes to this emotion. We often teach boys to repress sadness and commonly teach girls to linger on it. The result is men who may be afraid to cry, who may need anger management classes, and who may possibly struggle with expressing their feelings throughout their lives. On the other hand, women can go on and on about their sadness, cry their eyes out, ponder it, and turn right around to do it all over again. This does not necessarily mean that women may never need anger management classes or won't struggle with expressing their feelings. It just points to a difference in how adults frequently take contradictory approaches to teaching boys and girls how to manage their emotions. I believe that finding a happy medium would be a better approach.

Humans are not strangers to crying. It is a normal response for all children when overwhelmed by strong feelings. Little boys and girls cry with tears as a useful distress signal to engage the help of caretakers. Pain, hunger, and separation are typical causes of tears in infants. School-age children, like infants, may cry when they are hurt, but they also cry when they anticipate pain—such as knowing they're getting a shot at the doctor's office. They may also cry in response to emotional hurts, such as being rejected by peers or seeing a sad movie.

School-age children are usually better able than younger children to anticipate other people's reactions to their tears. They may cry to express guilt or remorse after they misbehave to ease their parents' anger and possibly to avoid punishment. (Can you relate? I can.) They may also try to avoid crying in front of certain peers they don't trust.

Then comes the social cost that psychologists say starts in about the first grade for children who cry in public. These costs usher in a "stiff upper lip" and the tendency to hide emotions. As it turns out, unless there is serious physical injury, a child is probably better off avoiding crying in front of peers and, if needed, postponing tears until a more private moment. I remember wanting so desperately to cry my eyes out on the first-grade playground when I wasn't chosen for the jump-rope team. I got my feelings hurt. But instead of crying when I was sure everyone would stare and make fun of me, I put my fingers in my mouth, moved back to the nearest hiding place, and waited for the bell to ring.

It is complicated, but unfortunately, through the years, we just haven't put much emphasis on learning how to understand and manage emotions. The question is, how many parents themselves were taught anything about emotions? My parents were wonderful Christians who struggled to lovingly do their best in dealing with whatever drama showed up as they went along raising five kids. I experienced hurt feelings as a child, but the truth is that I had no idea what emotions even were until high school when I ran head-on into my teen years. When that happened, my parents had all they could handle, working overtime with four daughters trying to quiet the storms and react to all the emotional challenges that came their way. Any teaching they did about emotions came mostly after the fact.

I often wonder what this must have been like for my little brother, Cal. He had four older sisters with their "silly girl" shenanigans, yet he was urged to act like a man and not be a "sissy." How did he express his emotions? He cried when he was little like the rest of us, but after he started school, I don't remember. He was usually quiet and smiled most of the time. Did he begin a life of suppressing his feelings, hiding his need to cry, and pushing away his pain? I wonder.

I have no special training in psychology, but since I have been intrigued by emotions for years and wanted to know more, I selected the topic for a special research project associated with my quest for a graduate degree in higher education. I was fortunate to be employed by a large educational organization that offered tuition reimbursement for studies at their colleges. Through the eleven years that I worked there in educational leadership, I succeeded in earning two graduate degrees that provided training for advancement within the company. A highlight of this experience was publishing my dissertation, which explored how college students operated in the online learning environment, which at that time was a very new educational platform.

My study found that students better connected with online lessons when they shared their feelings, opinions, and experiences in their online classes. This project heightened my awareness of the role that emotions play in life. The research inspired me to continue exploring the connection between thought and emotions and write this personal account of how emotions have affected my life.

Although various theories describe mechanisms leading to differential parenting of boys and girls, there is no consensus about the extent to which parents treat their sons and daughters differently.[1] I haven't undertaken a study to measure the existence of these occurrences; however, my personal observations and experiences support the claim that we absolutely *do* treat boys and girls differently. My question is, why not allow boys to express sadness when they feel it by having a good cry every now and then? I have found as a mother, grandmother, and even as a college administrator that too many guys repress their feelings and too many girls are overly expressive about their emotions. Can't we teach girls to not mull over their feelings so much? Where is the middle ground?

As you would probably expect with my background, I think it comes down to education. I believe that the answer involves meeting in the middle by creating a foundation built on education for both adults and children. This involves understanding that emotions are important and that it is imperative that we guide our children throughout their various stages of development. We should be sure to teach them to identify feelings and let them know that although all feelings are acceptable, all behavior is not. Parents and grandparents should set an example by talking to, listening to, and engaging with their boys and girls. And more than anything else, we ought to take time to show children where in the Bible God displays feelings and where He says that He cares about our feelings.[2] All of this will help build a strong foundation for our children based on God's abiding love for them.

These types of actions by parents and teachers help to nurture an important aspect of children's overall well-being—their *emotional intelligence*. Emotional intelligence is the ability to understand and control your own feelings and to understand the feelings of others and react to them in a suitable way.[3] Daniel Goleman, an expert on emotional intelligence, says that instead of purely cognitive abilities that are measured by conventional IQ tests, a definite set of emotional skills—your EQ—is what really matters for character, success, happiness, and lifelong achievement.[4]

Many experts agree with Goleman and consider EQ (Emotional Quotient) to be as important as IQ (Intelligence Quotient). Medical school admissions committees are increasingly considering noncognitive measures like emotional intelligence in evaluating potential applicants,[5] and the Emotional Intelligence Admission Essay (EIAE) scale is now commonly used in making admission decisions in health-care education.[6]

As the Bible makes clear, God has emotions. Jesus wept the most important tears ever shed. Considering these truths, I consider it a sacred responsibility to learn how the fundamentals of emotional intelligence align with Biblical concepts. In that spirit, Dr. Bob Kellemen explores the question, "What Does the Bible Teach About Our Emotions?" He begins by saying that if we are to live Christlike lives—godly lives—then we need to know God's perspective on emotions. We need a practical, Biblical theology of emotionality.[7]

We live in a fast-paced era of rapid change with increased demands on parents, grandparents, and educators. Even so, no matter how crazy busy we are, I sincerely believe applying principles of emotional intelligence that have been adapted to reflect Biblical perspectives can provide a solid, God-given foundation for meeting in the middle for our children as well as for ourselves.

SEVEN

Is Crying a Sign of Weakness?

There is a sacredness in tears. They are not the mark of weakness, but of power. They speak more eloquently than ten thousand tongues. They are the messengers of overwhelming grief, of deep contrition, and of unspeakable love.
—**Washington Irving**

A few years ago, I read and heard repeatedly on television that because U.S. Speaker of the House John Boehner wept on television, he appeared weak and unfit for his "dignified" Congressional role. Nonsense!

Many honorable souls and "dignified" individuals throughout history have shown the same tendency to cry. Abraham Lincoln wept often; the occasion of first hearing "The Battle Hymn of the Republic" was enough to make him sob. Ulysses S. Grant wept when he received the news that Lincoln, who had been his friend and champion, had been assassinated. In 1789, when George Washington took the presidential oath of office, Chancellor Robert B. Livingston turned to the crowd and loudly exclaimed, "Long Live George Washington, President of the United States!" The enormous crowd watching the momentous occasion erupted in praise and applause. Washington bowed repeatedly as he wiped tears from his eyes.[1]

For many people, the consummate image of "dignity" will forever be Sir Winston Churchill. The notion of the British stiff upper lip was conceived by the Victorians and was especially predominant in the upper classes, where it was considered demeaning to show emotions openly. The British Empire has long been known for expecting their officers and gentlemen to abandon personal feelings in favor of remaining calm and collected under all circumstances. Yet Winston Churchill, an upper-class British Army officer, was well-known for his emotions. Given his extremely romantic imagination and empathetic nature, along with his aristocratic lack of regard for what others thought of him, if he felt like crying, well, "by jove," he just did.[2]

I like the sound of that. Surrendering our weaknesses—and we all most assuredly have them—to God allows Him to enter our lives in miraculous ways. My surrender of weaknesses involved letting go of my desire to control things. This included controlling my tears. I had developed a sense that if I tried harder, did the absolute best I could, and never gave up, I could make good things happen. I would make speeches about it and was proud of this commitment to being focused and driven to accomplish my goals. My attitude did bring successes that I fooled myself into thinking were all about my having taken control. However, somewhere along the way, after falling down many times and having a hard time getting back to being an "in control" winner, I gave up. In the past, that statement would have been nearly impossible for me to say or write, but I now proudly admit that I gave up. I gave in and surrendered my control, my life, and myself to my LORD Jesus Christ.

What a relief! I am free to be me—me with my strengths *and* my weaknesses. I am free to make mistakes and free to be weak where God intended me to be weak. That was my epiphany, and it is the obvious but somehow elusive message that I love to share. God intended for me to have weaknesses and to be just who I am—No More, No Less. We read in 1 Samuel 16:7, "The LORD does not look at the things people look at. People look at the outward appearance, but The LORD looks at the heart." He made us, He knows us, and He loves our weaknesses. Giving up my constant need to control things and giving my heart to Him has opened the door to His filling my life with the amazing joy of letting go. It's an old saying, but it's true nonetheless: "Let go and let God." I am much stronger now. I've come a long way in my journey to give up my need for control and in my quest to conquer my limitations and my tears. Through weakness, God provides strength.

Yes, the media has a way of inflicting strong criticism on national leaders who weep openly on television. Ironically, the famously calm and collected media legend Walter Cronkite, the CBS Evening News anchor known as "the most trusted man in America," is perhaps particularly remembered for his brief departure from that composure. Cronkite openly struggled to keep from crying and later admitted to "choking up" when his voice filled with emotion on November 22, 1963, as he interrupted *As the World Turns* to break the news that President John F. Kennedy had been shot.[3]

While news anchors like Cronkite have historically been

known for their stoicism, Anderson Cooper has become the perfect example of one with a more emotive style. In 2005, while talking to a group of desperate-looking evacuees in New Orleans after Hurricane Katrina hit, Cooper's emotions spilled over, and tears ran down his face as the camera rolled. Cooper has since been praised for showing genuine humanity.[4] Could it be that perhaps the winds of change have granted a show of compassion, benevolence, and kindness for our leaders and the "dignified"?

Queen Elizabeth II is a highly respected leader who exemplifies dignified women who have succeeded on the world stage. As a woman of strength with a heritage to represent, she carries the responsibility for her country and her lineage with pride and rarely is seen crying in public. In an episode of the third season of *The Crown*, a Netflix historical drama, the Queen admits she pretended to cry in public. This stirred speculation that she might be "hard-hearted." Imagine that. Evidently, many people think leaders, particularly women leaders, should show their emotions. Whatever the case, the truth is that Queen Elizabeth does cry in public. She cried in December 1997 when her Royal Yacht Britannia was shut down. In 2002, she wiped away a tear while visiting the Field of Remembrance at Westminster Abbey, and in 2016, she was visibly upset when attending a service for fallen soldiers of the Duke of Lancaster's Regiment.[5]

On the other hand, women have had issues with being considered weak throughout history. While the phrase "the weaker sex" was the title of a 1948 British film about life on the home front during World War II, it is primarily associated with women and has been throughout history. Charles Dickens wrote of the weaker sex in *The Old Curiosity Shop*: "Now, the ladies being together under these circumstances, it was extremely natural that the discourse should turn upon the propensity of mankind to tyrannize over the weaker sex, and the duty that developed upon the weaker sex to resist that tyranny and assert their rights and dignity."[6]

If you search for the idiom "weaker sex" in the *Free Dictionary* by Farlex, you find *female sex*.[7] We could excuse this by accepting that females are generally physically weaker than males, but the question here is whether females are considered weaker because they are more prone to cry than males. Or is crying considered a sign of weakness because it is associated with that old idiom "the weaker sex"? Perhaps. After all, it has been established that women cry more frequently than men.

Ad Vingerhoets, the tear expert and author of the book *Why Only Humans Weep: Unravelling the Mysteries of Tears*,[8] is one of the few researchers currently studying tears triggered by feelings. His work suggests that the stereotype about women crying more than men is true: women cry thirty to sixty-four times a year, whereas men cry just six to seventeen times per year. Interestingly, science takes the stage when Vingerhoets suggests that women often have shallow tear ducts, which fill up more quickly so that tears spill over. This appears to be true for most women when compared to men. The tear duct issue and relevant hormonal changes that happen around puberty provide at least a partial physiological explanation as to why men tend to cry less often than women.

Now you might be thinking, "But what about those people

who cry at the drop of a hat?" While that is an old expression, we all have known people, both men and women, who totally fit that description. I love tears, but too much of a good thing is always a pity. Think about the effects of eating too much chocolate, walking ten miles every day, or even having hundreds of passwords! An excessive amount of weeping can not only be harmful, but it can make others uncomfortable and undermine sincerity.

Crybabies have never been especially popular. Do they really have that much to cry about? Most of us have vivid memories of being scolded not to be a crybaby. My goodness, back then it sounded like the worst thing in the world! The fact is that we may have used that same expression ourselves to stop the tears. Tears hold a great deal of power. Managing that power can be a challenge, but if it comes at the expense of repressing emotions, it may be too great a price to pay.

In his article "The Wisdom of Crying," Dr. Gary Brown asserts that crying is an important part of our mental health. He states that crying is not a sign of weakness; instead, when we cry, we are simply showing our normal humanity. He suggests that the ability to cry shows a certain strength of personality and indicates that you feel more freedom to express yourself. Dr. Brown goes on to say that constantly living behind the "I've got it together mask" will only leave a person emotionally isolated and alone.[9]

In my quest to understand my tears, I have often thought of the apostle Paul, who repeatedly spoke of his mysterious "affliction" and was prone to weep. For example, he wrote in 2 Corinthians 2:4, "For out of much affliction and anguish of heart I wrote unto you with many tears; not that ye should be grieved, but that ye might know the love which I have more abundantly unto you."

Afflictions have been a part of the substance of history and of so many leaders' lives, from Franklin D. Roosevelt to John F. Kennedy to Ronald Reagan. If shedding tears is an affliction and thereby a weakness, I have concluded that what we need in this old world is more weakness. Again, we are reminded that through weakness God provides strength. "But he said to me, 'My grace is sufficient for you, for my power is made perfect in weakness.' Therefore, I will boast all the more gladly about my weaknesses, so that Christ's power may rest on me" (2 Corinthians 12:9). My desire for control and my weeping weaknesses are now in God's hands, and I am comforted by these words from C. S. Lewis: "Affliction is often that thing which prepares an ordinary person for some sort of an extraordinary destiny."[10]

EIGHT

The Beauty of Tears

Beauty of whatever kind, in its supreme development, invariably excites the sensitive soul to tears.

—Edgar Allen Poe

As you know by now, I am a weeper with a reputation for misting up. I'm often frustrated by crying at the most inconvenient times, but beauty abounds in our tears. They go together, like when I'm at church and the beauty of the music and inspirational words touches me deeply and I weep while others likely look at me thinking *poor thing*. I not only cry at church but also when I watch sad or happy movies, when I see someone being especially kind to someone else, when snowflakes cover my hair and eyelashes, when I watch a little child play with a lovable puppy, and when a friend sends me a touching birthday card. And I can count on crying during my daily devotional time that is all about beautiful thoughts. Invariably, with the glow and the goose bumps come the tears. These lovely thoughts and heartfelt tears combine to produce moments straight from heaven. They are connections to God.

Recently, when I was running late and all set to head out

the door, I had second thoughts. I stopped to make time for my daily devotional. As usual, my tears appeared, and I was left with smudged makeup and puffy eyes. But this time was different. Something special came with the uninvited tears. God, who has heard my prayers asking for relief from these annoying tears for many, many years, not only whispered to me during this morning quiet time about the goodness of my tears, He assured me that they belonged there, running down my face. Of course, they did, and they do! Why had I never seen it that way?

Truth is, tears are such a miraculous part of who we are! They are a gift—and one we carry with us from birth until death. This gift is something of a mystery, and yet, oh what a blessing, to whimper, to weep, to sob with anguish. All tears are divine gifts—pearls of salt that fall from our lashes to serve us throughout our lives in many kinds of different situations.

After that pivotal moment when God spoke to me, I began to embrace my tears. I resolved to no longer be embarrassed by them, to no longer strain to keep them at bay. Let them flow. God has ordained them.

The next time I slathered all that "great" moisturizer and makeup on my face, I remembered Edgar Allen Poe's observation that it is often beauty that excites our souls to tears. And I thought, *Is this a cause-and-effect thing?* Now consider that! Could it be that my tears, the ones I have shed and *lost* because of the beauty found in God's word, have been *absorbed* to enhance my beauty? Could they be a "magic salty potion" to give beauty, perhaps vanquish my wrinkles, and bring a glow to my countenance?

The next time my tears flow, that is exactly how I plan to receive them, as sweet gifts that roll down my face, make me lovelier and, dare I say, fresher and more youthful. Yes, yes, perhaps tears help accomplish all the desires we women bring to our dressing table.

Suggestion: The next time tears roll down your cheeks, delicately pat them into your face, all around your eyes, your cheeks, and even your mouth. Do this with a gentle touch, one reserved for something we rarely do, which is showing love for ourselves. What an epiphany to have been given this magic potion to relish and "absorb." Out of the way, Bobbi Brown and Kiehl's creams! My tears are all I need!

I love the thought that tears enhance our outer beauty, but more importantly, could they enhance inner beauty and our connection to God? In her book *Lit from Within*, Victoria Moran gives daily tips for boosting awareness of your inner beauty, illustrating how true sparkle comes from a sense of wholeness. "Beauty isn't skin deep—it's soul deep," she says.[1] Her approach to a strong self-image and loving self-care is grounded in spiritual common sense and the marriage of body and soul. She writes, "You start by lighting up your life—and before you know it, you're lighting up the room."[2]

Paying attention gives us the sensor, the vibe, the sheer magical sense of knowing inner beauty and its connection to God. Beauty that we can see is enjoyable, especially when it stares back at us in the mirror and we are pleased with ourselves, but is it authentic? The Bible instructs us that "charm is deceptive, and beauty is fleeting, but a woman who fears the Lord is to be praised" (Proverbs 31:30).

After all, think how very unreliable outer beauty can be. I had crushes on handsome guys throughout school and idolized "cute" girls who later turned out to be bullies and brats. On the inside, they were definitely less than beautiful or handsome. Inner beauty is not as sly as outer beauty, not as adept at creating a false image and hiding iniquity. It is, however, elusive, and it often hides waiting for you to discover it, not with your eyes, but with your heart. It takes "attention" to recognize inner beauty; a glance will not do. Neither a stare nor loads of pictures is enough. It takes deep attentiveness to wait, be still, and become aware of your connection to God. It's all part of tuning in to inner beauty that is not revealed at first glance.

Have you known someone who was a true beauty, inside and out? I have, and I loved her with all of my heart. To look at her was to think, *How could she be so perfect?* Without makeup and even with her hair flying in all directions from chasing after five kids, my mother, Mary Frances, had unadorned and lovely outer beauty.

Nevertheless, it was her inner beauty that earned her abiding admiration and love from all who knew her. Such is the nature of a true beauty. As a little girl, I would gaze at her, wanting so much to be just like her in every way. Later, when there was no hope that I was ever going to look like my auburn-haired, brown-eyed, gorgeous mother, I decided it was okay. She dressed me in pink to go with my blond hair and turquoise blue eyes and made me feel every bit as beautiful just the way I was. She took me to church almost every time the door opened, taught me to love Jesus, and gave me so much of herself and her love. That's the magic, you see. The magic of a true beauty is the gift of beauty shared from the inside—from a beautiful heart. As the Bible says, "Your beauty should not come from outward adornment, such as elaborate hairstyles and the wearing of gold jewelry or fine clothes. Rather, it should be that of your inner self, the unfading beauty of a gentle and quiet spirit, which is of great worth in God's sight." (1 Peter 3:3–4).

Beauty repeatedly shows up in the Bible as God is revealed (1 Peter 3:3–4, 1 Samuel 16:7, Ecclesiastes 3:11, James 1:23, Proverbs 31:30), but we are making a mistake if we interpret that as meaning "beautiful" is about outward perfection. The truth is that God works through those we don't expect, blesses those we think are unworthy, and lifts up those who are often way off our radar. We ought to be on the lookout for inner beauty and its connection to God. Ask yourself who in your life might have something remarkable to reveal to you about Him.

As the poet Edgar Allen Poe said, beauty of whatever kind does excite the sensitive soul. I wish you lots of attentiveness in your quest for beauty—inner beauty, that is. Physical beauty, after all, might take your breath away and leave you with a lovely image to remember. But what about the beauty, the "inner beauty," that is God's gift in so much of what we experience every day? Think of your reaction to a poignant poem, a rousing rhapsody, or a spectacular symphony. Or consider spoken words that make you swoon, make you cry, or drive you crazy with delight? Why do you react that way? It's not a conscious reaction; it's an involuntary reaction to your inner connection with God. It's God's beauty, which we cannot always see with our eyes but know inwardly. Yes, it's the beauty we recognize in the people we love, and it satisfies the yearning of our hearts and souls. All of these are beautiful gifts that, *like tears,* can easily lay claim to having and even, perhaps, being the essence of inner beauty.

It is humbling. How do we recognize the difference? We know in our hearts that what the world sees and what we see in the mirror is not what God sees and not what we know about ourselves! The secret may elude us for a while as we grow up and become women, but the winner, after all, turns out to be beauty we cannot see with our eyes. But when we pay attention ... yes, there it is. We can recognize inner beauty and its connection to God with our hearts and feel it in our goose bumps and chills. That is beauty! Pay attention. It is all around you and your tears will give it away ... your soul knows.

NINE
Being True to Yourself

Authenticity is a collection of choices that we have to make every day. It's about the choice to show up and be real. The choice to be honest. The choice to let our true selves be seen.

—Brené Brown

Did you ever second-guess yourself or try too hard and cry yourself to sleep? You hide in your room, hit the pillow again and again, and turn an incident over in your mind until you fall asleep sobbing and hoping to awaken as that "other girl." You know, the wonderful, perfect girl who does all the right things and always looks "just right."

It was the summer between seventh and eighth grade. I usually spent the summer playing outside with my sisters, especially Alice. We would swing on the giant swing set in our backyard, pretend to be cowboys and Indians, and ride on long tomato stakes from Daddy's garden. We made mud pies, played hide-and-seek, and rode our bikes around the neighborhood. The hours crept by until it was suppertime and we flew into the house with dirty fingernails, bare, blackened feet, and scrapes on our knees from all kinds of accidents, scuffles, and fun, pure fun.

This summer would be different because I was growing up and seventh-grade geometry had beaten me down—talk about scrapes and crying! Geometry and I had a major scuffle and geometry had won. I had received a D for my final grade. My self-identity was severely bruised. I was humiliated and ashamed that I had to go to summer school to take algebra, but I had to have the credits.

I rode the bus every day, which turned out to be fun. At first, algebra and I got along great, and I enjoyed the entire idea of walking away from the geometry disaster and moving on, no turning back, with relief and success under my belt. You would think that would be *the* big memory I carried away from that summer—the B-plus I earned in Algebra, a huge success! Not so. Instead, as if it were yesterday, I can remember accidentally sitting on the bus one day next to Carol Anne, a popular, cute brunette with her bubble haircut (all the rage), saddle oxfords, and pricey-looking clothes. I was extremely intimidated. I can still feel the awkwardness and yucky taste of fear. I wanted so completely to be just like her, to go places she went and be in her social group. That would be the ultimate achievement, to be accepted by this girl. This had been my dream since elementary school when I stood alone on the playground and wondered why they did not ask me to jump rope with them.

This clear memory of the fear and my nervous attempt to sound cool and talk like I thought popular girls would talk haunts me to this day. It is so real that I can almost see her look of condescension and veiled, ever-so-slight look of ridicule. It was as if she had been suddenly called upon to "be nice," as her mother would say, and act like she should toward the don't-know-any-better folks. I was mortified as I got off the bus.

And yet, I was still so full of hope that she liked me and would tell everyone how nice I was and to include me in their group and all their fun. I never heard from her or her friends. If I saw them, they smiled nicely (that "nice" thing again) but went on their way, not at all interested in knowing me or accepting me. It broke my heart. Day after day, I would hide in my room, sobbing and feeling sorry for myself, until I finally got tired of it and gave up. By the time eighth grade started up, I went from settling for being "unpopular me" to deciding to be the best me possible. This involved something of a makeover with unveiling a new "look" (a bubble haircut, of course), joining several clubs, volunteering for just about everything out there, and making better grades.

The real change came with a new attitude. After all, the truth about that whole episode was that the *perfect girl* did not know me at all. That wasn't me talking to her there on the bus. It was someone I was pretending to be, and you know what they say about recognizing a fake a mile away. That nervous, false pretender was unable to relax, take a breath, be quiet, and just be myself. On top of that, the *perfect* girl was a total stranger in every way. I didn't know her heart or care whether I would even like being around her. I judged her and her friends by how they looked and how people looked at them.

I learned a valuable lesson. But I still carry that awful memory and it makes me feel so small and stupid. When it comes to mind, all over again, I am that fearful, tense teenager trying too hard, and I can barely breathe, even though it was all those years ago. I remember trying to be better, when better was right there in my heart and soul. "Better" was being re-laxed and easy—being authentic. "Better" was about accepting myself and being content with being liked for being me. While this happened so long ago, it's a memory with a message that is true for us at every age. I have evolved through the years into a "what you see, is what you get" kind of person. It has paid off with so many rich blessings: treasured friendships, jobs that were the right fit, opportunities to serve others, and, above all, peace of mind. As Dolly Parton said, "Find out who you are and do it on purpose."

And why not? When courage forsakes you and you wish you were (and desperately try to be) someone else, you have turned your back on the best friend you will ever have: *the real you*. That friend is waiting quietly, watching you cry for all the wrong reasons. Make time to get to know yourself so the real you can shine through. That person inside is your magi-cal, unique spirit, your forever best friend. Don't leave her out; don't ever let her down.

You are made in the image of God with a divine spirit. Get-ting to know yourself starts with recognizing that you are a rare and distinctive masterpiece. Science tells us that each of us has forty-six chromosomes. Half of those come from your father and the rest from your mother. Your unique combination of chromosomes determines everything from the color of your eyes to whether you are left-handed, have a mean backhand, and even the number of hairs of your head that God counts.

All that you are is not just about what you inherited from your earthly parents. Your identity in large part is about what you inherited from your Heavenly Father, and this includes your inner spirit, your inner beauty, and your destiny. Dr. Wayne Dyer suggested that honoring our Divine spirit should always be our first thought. He taught that teaching our outer self to accept the unlimited power of our inner spirit would allow us to reach unimaginable heights.[1]

TEN

Repentant Tears

The remembrance of sin committed is the Holy Spirit's frequent, if not constant method of bringing men to weep over their wrong-doing and to turn from it.

—C. H Spurgeon

One of my sister Janice's favorite stories of our childhood together is about a time when I was the evil big sister. I've never heard her tell it when I wasn't present, but I am sure she makes it quite a colorful tale. She is a talented storyteller, and when I am not around to dampen her "you are not going to believe this" spirit, well, I can only imagine how absolutely horrible I must seem to be. Finally, right here and now, I have a chance to tell the story from my perspective for one and all to read. I guess it is but a minor sin in the grand scheme of things, but it remains a vivid memory I continue to recall and contemplate with eyes that see a side of me I am reluctant to admit exists.

I am nine years older than my sister, and from the time I was nine until about fifteen, Janice was often my responsibility. For example, when she was five or six, I would take her to the swimming pool—charged with making sure she didn't drown. This sounds a little terse, but the truth is, she was a handful, especially at the swimming pool where she had total confidence that she could swim better than any frog, fish, or dolphin out there. Much of her swimming was underwater, which meant I could not talk to friends or casually be on standby while she swam. I had to *watch* her every minute. She would disappear frequently and, honestly, I think she loved to play the game of "let's scare big sister" as often as possible. I would get so angry, which just made her giggle and jump in the pool for another attempt at holding her breath for as long as possible.

We had a close relationship, with me babysitting and taking care of her much of the time, but it was more like being her watchdog than her sweet big sister. She always called me bossy, and I certainly earned the title. Since my persuasive techniques were not especially refined, being pushy, overbearing, and controlling were my tools of choice.

On an especially boring day when she was about five years old, I got the bright idea to have a little fun with her. She was playing in her room when I ran in, threw my arms around her, and begged her to come with me to hide quickly. I acted terror-stricken. She believed every bit of it and ran with me to hide in the back corner of Mother's closet. I closed the door and we huddled on the floor in the dark behind Mother's dresses and on top of her shoes while I spun my tale of terror: Martians had landed in our hometown. I had heard about it on the radio, I told her, and they were headed in the direction of our house. We had to be very still and as quiet as little mice or they might find us and eat us or take us off in their spaceships to their planet for spooky experiments.

My charade ended when I watched her disintegrate into a weeping, quivering little puddle of a baby sister. The realization of how my *fun* had not been fun at all left me forlorn and wanting to hide. So, acting like it was "no big deal," I told her the truth. She cried loudly, threw things at me, and stormed away. I went to my room (my hideout) and, although she later told me that she never tattled, I began years of effort trying to put the entire episode behind me.

Isn't this the way it is with our sins, whether they are tiny or immense? We push them down whenever they make an appearance, again and again. Out of sight, out of mind, right? But somewhere in the dark, way in the "back of our minds," they hang out just waiting for the day when you might bring them into the light. Then it happens: a chance for repentance. Even a years-ago nasty trick can bring tears. Lots of words describe those tears, including disappointment, regret, shame, and sorrow. These words are the reality of repentance. As Horace Mann once said, "When a child can be brought to tears, and not for fear of punishment, but for repentance, he needs no chastisement. When the tears begin to flow from the grief of that conduct, you can be sure there is an angel nestling in their heart."[1]

One of the greatest examples of a repentant heart is found in the Bible. Simon Peter betrays Jesus, the man he loves deeply. This happens not once but three times. He runs away and hides. He does everything he can to push the betrayal out of his mind, to explain it away, to "make it okay." Nothing works. Finally, with repentant tears, he crumbles in disgust with himself. He admits, accepts, and perhaps even exaggerates the ugly truth of what he has done. He is guilty, and even his tears cannot change that truth.

His confession brings a change. It was a miraculous change that Jesus foretold, a change that will forever be the story God shares with you and me to "make it okay." Jesus forgave him. What was the miraculous change? Despite his betrayal, Peter believed and repented, and his life was never the same. He became God's special chosen one, the Rock on whom His church is built. "He saith unto them, 'But whom say ye that I am?' And Simon Peter answered and said, 'Thou art the Christ, the Son of the living God.' And Jesus answered and said unto him, 'Blessed art thou, Simon Barjona: for flesh and blood hath not revealed it unto thee, but my Father which is in heaven. And I say also unto thee, that thou art Peter, and upon this rock I will build my church; and the gates of hell shall not prevail against it" (Matthew 16:15–18 KJV).

Coming to terms with our sins, in whatever way God uses to get our attention, is an opportunity for repentance. Each time that memory moves from the back of your mind and peeks its head around the corner to remind you, it's giving you a chance to bring the sin from the darkness into the blessed light by your admittance, acceptance, and repentance.

One of the most famous and prolific English weepers was a fifteenth-century mystic called Margery Kempe. She was an extreme weeper, and for her, it was a religious act. She is said to have called it an act of penance, of compunction—penitence about sins and also of compassion with the suffering of others, especially the suffering of Christ. Thomas Dix, director of the Centre for the History of the Emotions at Queen Mary University of London, explains that in medieval Catholicism, weeping was not only about acting religious, it was a duty. By weeping, one displayed compassion and connection to the suffering at the center of the Christian religion.[2]

What does repentance look like, and how does it feel? When I first heard the word, I was confused and felt sure it was a place I did not want to be. Perhaps that is why we often take so long to go there. It sounds daunting, frightening, and much like a sure road to punishment.

The years-long effort at putting the little sister episode behind me ended recently. I finally gave in to the memory when it moved to the front of my mind in living color. A couple of years ago, while on vacation in Charleston, South Carolina, with our husbands, Janice and I left the guys watching their beloved football game to go out on the balcony for time together. It was a perfect summer evening with a soft breeze, chirping crickets, and the heavenly scent of all sorts of Southern flowers. It was exactly right for sharing stories, catching up, and reminiscing about growing up together. I was relaxed, and before I knew it, I reminded her of that time in Mother's closet. At first, she was very still and didn't say a thing for what seemed like two hours. When she finally spoke, she said she had never forgotten and admitted that it was one of her worst memories from childhood. *Cringe! Look away! Change the subject?* No, I told myself, stay with it and admit you were wrong, ask her to forgive you, and try to understand. I did all of that, and she listened. I had secretly hoped she would make light of it, but instead, I felt a renewed sense of guilt. And yet, what a relief for both of us to have finally shared our feelings with each other.

After all those years, we were able to confess that, despite childhood slights, we do genuinely love each other. My tears, tears of relief and loving tears for my little sister, came later when I was alone. Those memories and that guilt no longer hide in the background, and I trust we both understood after we hugged tightly when we said goodbye.

I think she has forgiven me, but I know my Savior has forgiven me. My repentant tears have definitely had other opportunities to emerge and for far deeper, darker sins. Perhaps with this experience with my sister, God gave me a chance to learn that repentance is a gift that comes from His Holy Spirit, right there in our hearts, and it is more about love than I ever understood.

"Repent ye therefore, and be converted, that your sins may be blotted out, when the times of refreshing shall come from the presence of the LORD" (Acts 3:19).

There is something special about closets. As in my case, they are often about secrets and hiding. Consider for a moment what the Bible teaches about closets: "But thou, when thou prayest, enter into thy closet, and when thou hast shut thy door, pray to thy Father which is in secret; and thy Father which seeth in secret shall reward thee openly" (Matthew 6:6 KJV). And then there is Dr. Bryce Klabunde, pastor of College Avenue Baptist Church in San Diego, who describes repentant people as those willing to confess all their sins, not just the sins that got them in trouble. When discussing signs of genuine repentance, he asserts that people who desire purity are completely honest about their lives with no more secrets. And to bring home the point, he reminds us that a house isn't really clean until you open every closet and sweep every corner.[3]

ELEVEN

No Two Tears Are Alike

Cry. Forgive. Learn. Move on. Let your tears water the seeds of your future happiness.
—Steve Maraboli

Lettie Cowman was onto something in her beloved daily devotional *Streams in the Desert*, when she wrote that "nearly all God's jewels are crystallized tears."[1] I rarely remember my dreams, but not too long ago, I woke with an exceptionally vivid memory of a sweet, sweet dream. It included lovely curly hair sprinkled with snowflakes and a beautiful yet blurry face revealing cheeks adorned with traces of tears—in captivating dried white sprinkles. Now, having skied every winter in the Rocky Mountains for over thirty years, I have developed a deep love for snowflakes, and that dream with those sprinkles spoke to me of a magic connection between snowflakes and tears. Let's explore the magic together.

First, let's consider snowflakes. In the online series *Everyday Mysteries*, The Library of Congress explored the question: Is it true that no two snow crystals are alike? After a fascinating explanation, the resounding scientific consensus was that it is very unlikely for two large complex snow crystals to be identical in molecular structure and appearance.[2] Most people believe that no two snowflakes are exactly alike and, as a skier, I learned this in a delightful way. I often spent time in a lift chair riding up a mountain examining snowflakes on my dark gloves or jacket. If you look closely, you can see the differences in them even when wearing goggles. Once, when we had the good fortune to ski in Canada on the Whistler Blackcomb Mountain in British Columbia, we experienced snowflakes the size of a dime—well, maybe the size of a Cheerio or a baby's button. Whatever the case, they were bigger than usual. It was amazing to see them on your clothes, your hat, your nose, and your eyelashes before they melted. They were perfectly sized, exquisite jewels, each unique and vanishing as you watched and wondered. I never saw two that looked the same. Why should anything be so beautiful for such a brief time? There should be a way to capture them, keep them, and never let them go. I believe they are truly each a one-of-a-kind disappearing treasure.

Interestingly, after studying snowflakes' differences under a microscope, scientists have determined that their appearance varies depending on environmental factors, such as the temperature, air currents, and humidity conditions surrounding their creation. Most snowflakes are six-sided, with those created in warmer temperatures often appearing smoother and less geometric. While magnifying snowflakes helps scientists learn more about the conditions present while the snow was being formed, it still doesn't explain how they fall all around you at the same time and in the same location, yet they are all different. I am amazed, but along with everything else He does for us, God is best at making us wonder![3]

Similarly, for over eight years, Rose-Lynn Fisher used her microscopes to explore the unseen realm of emotions in her study of tears. In her published visual investigation of tears, *The Topography of Tears*,[4] she shares images of tears photographed through a digital microscope mounted on a vintage optical microscope. As with snowflakes, many variables influenced the diversity among the tear images, including whether the tear was air-dried or compressed, the volume of tear fluid, the chemical/biological variations, and the microscope and camera settings, along with how Fisher processed and printed the photographs. Various emotions are represented in Fisher's study of tears, and each image differs dramatically from the others. Each tear image, whether a tear of elation, sorrow, frustration, rejection, or another emotion, is unique and distinctive. Interestingly, these mysterious images resemble topographical images of our world, our universe. Fisher compares shedding tears to shedding old skin, noting that, like one drop of an ocean, it's as if each tear contains a miniature version of the collective human experience.[5]

Returning to magic and the notion of crystallized tears, do you suppose that if we froze our tears, we could create snowflakes? Using my imagination, I like to think I could, and I love the idea of creating my own personal snowflakes. But Cowman was talking about God's jewels being crystallized tears. While snowflakes are heavenly jewels in oh-so-many ways, I believe that Cowman's notion of God's jewels being crystallized tears was inspired and wonderfully beautiful. Indeed, it tells of the valuable, unique outcomes we experience after walking through life—especially tragedy, sorrow, deep depression, or grief.

My cousin Holly's years of crystallized tears truly were a gift of God's jewels. She suffered through a long, lonely, and frightening separation from her husband. He walked away and left her with only debt and painful memories. She refused to take any action against him until slowly, as time moved on, she found courage. With help, she gradually found light, and confidence came back into her life. Through it all, she held on and prayed. And through it all, God was with her. Then came the tragic news that her husband had died.

Despite his desertion, she was devastated and heartbroken when notified of his death. But with that dreadful news came God's jewel—His gift of a new life. As the widow, she would be receiving benefits from her estranged husband's Social Security and his company pension. She paid her debts, moved to live near her daughter, and now spends precious time with her four grandkids. She found closure and was finally free of the pain. Holly will always mourn his loss, but the divorce that she desperately sought so that she could survive never happened. Thank the Lord!

TWELVE

Tears and the Green-Eyed Monster

O beware, my lord, of jealousy; It is the green-eyed monster which doth mock the meat it feeds on.

—William Shakespeare

The "green-eyed monster" is an idiomatic expression in English that describes an overwhelming sense of jealousy. The phrase personifies jealousy as a beast, indicating just how destructive it can be as an emotion. William Shakespeare originated the term in *Othello* when Iago tries to manipulate Othello by suggesting that his wife, Desdemona, is having an affair. Iago plants the seeds of jealousy in Othello's mind using the now famous expression. Subsequently, the color green became associated with the emotions of jealousy and envy, and from that, the expression "green with envy" was derived.

As you know, I have a special fondness for tears and eyes, and I am certain they are the doorway to a person's heart—the place where emotions reside. Science tells us that eyes grow rapidly after birth. Then, within a few months, the growth becomes linear and continues until a person reaches around 20 to 21 years of age, while their weight continues to increase over the course of a lifetime.[1] Additionally, the American Academy of Ophthalmology (AAO) says most babies have the eye color that will last their lifetime by the time they are about nine months old.[2] The unique color of a person's eyes is important. It gives me pleasure to notice how the coloring that distinguishes an individual's features, like hair color and skin tone, all seem to come together around the color of their eyes.

I can acknowledge that I have blue-green eyes, but I prefer to call them blue or turquoise. Approximately 2 percent of the worldwide population has green eyes.[3] And although having green eyes is rare, the association with a "green-eyed monster" makes me uneasy. This is largely because jealousy has been chasing me for many years, nipping at my heels and inflicting many wounds.

This started when I was a two-year-old beauty. Of course, I do not remember details, but I recall having an overwhelming certainty of love and comfort and feeling so joyful and happy to be my precious, perfect self. I recognize this sensation primarily because of how it was altered so suddenly when *she* came into my life. The contrast drew such a sharp distinction.

I could write reams about her—my sister Alice Frances. A true beauty with big brown eyes, auburn hair, and such a sweet spirit, she had many qualities to envy. In fact, it was like having Elizabeth Taylor (back then) or Salma Hayek (today) as my closest friend and bunking buddy. My natural beauty and charm seemed to fade in comparison to Alice Frances, and that soon became my very favorite activity and sport: comparison.

I started crying tears of jealousy early in my life. As early as three or four, I remember crying to my mother and complaining that she did not love me as much as Alice. This could be sorrowful weeping or screaming and boohooing when Alice, two years younger, got her way and I did not. My daddy also appeared to favor her at times. When things went wrong, it seemed that he usually blamed me. I would rant, rave, and cry. It was so exasperating. I never was able to shake the jealousy; after all, I could not change my eyes, my hair, or my nose. But what I could do was try as hard as possible to outdo Alice in every other way. I somehow did succeed in some ways, and it was gratifying, at least for a time, but it also almost completely ruined my life. Jealousy can do that.

All this may sound melodramatic, especially since we are talking about tears, but it is not an exaggeration. I was a college girl with no boyfriend. George, my sweetheart since the tenth grade, had gone to college, found another love, and married her. My heart was broken. During my sophomore year, I met Ralph when I was working during the Christmas holidays in the men's department of the nearby Belk store. He was not exactly my type at the time, but he was an attractive college football player, and I developed a crush on him. Before long, we began seeing each other, and we dated regularly for a little over a year. Along the way, Ralph met Alice, and I sensed that he had a keen interest in her. He seemed to try to get her attention, and I thought he flirted with her. Having lived with this sibling jealousy for quite a while, I was uncomfortable when it came to competing with Alice. That, along with my lack of confidence in my feelings for Ralph, kept me awake at night and doing whatever possible to ignore the jealous feelings. When I finally grew sick of it, I jumped at the chance to take a job as a flight attendant in Texas, hoping to put jealousy and Ralph behind me.

I lived in an apartment in Houston with four other flight attendants and worked a crazy rookie schedule of flying back-to-back trips. There were lots of fun times, but lots of lonely times too, and Ralph kept calling and calling. When I got tired of the schedule and tired of being lonely, I transferred back to Memphis and Ralph. There, I ran right into the green-eyed monster big time. I did not want to believe that my very own sister might have been going out with my ex while I was away, but the evidence was pretty clear when I caught them together a couple of times looking somewhat affectionate. However, they claimed they were "just friends." Confronting them was not my tactic, and I had no real proof. Instead, Ralph and I got engaged, and I started planning a wedding. When Ralph broke off the engagement, I called Daddy. He called Ralph, and before I knew what was happening, they had become partners in a business deal and our engagement was back on. All the while, I wasn't even sure I loved the guy anymore. But guess what was driving this train to disaster? That's right: jealousy. I was not about to stand still and watch Ralph and Alice end up together. How totally embarrassing; what could I possibly say to explain that to my friends?

The Lord absolutely gave me every chance to back out, but on it went and, before long, I was too far in. The night before the wedding, when a thunderstorm literally shook the walls with warnings and lightning bolts screamed through the sky, I hid away and cried my eyes out knowing what a mistake I was making, but there was just no turning back.

Less than a year later, Ralph and I broke up. He had wandering eyes, so it was on-again, off-again until we eventually divorced as quickly as possible and went our separate ways. Thankfully, throughout it all, Alice and I remained close, but the damage still haunts me. What stupid decisions. How could I have been so ignorant? Jealousy is vicious. It can laugh in your face while your life falls apart and tears are your only companion. I often wonder whether perhaps jealous tears as a little girl were an early warning that I would always be vulnerable to the green-eyed monster. Would it have mattered had I recognized the signs? Kevlar vests and all the other armor you can muster are needed when jealousy is your opponent. It can be a serious battle.

Irony gets the last word. To further complicate things, I could never and will never love anyone as much as I loved my sweet sister Alice during our years together. In many ways, the pain and the tears were all about her.

I lost her to cancer thirty years ago. The buckets of tears I shed then brought back so many memories of life with Alice—sharing all our secrets, her happiness to be with me anywhere, her rubbing my back when we were little girls snuggling up together while the attic fan blew a lovely breeze across our bed, our dancing and singing on top of the picnic table. I could go on and on, but these memories in some strange way taught me that my jealousy for her may very well have really been about love.

To have been so deeply jealous that I would step into the mess I lived through involved two strong emotions—love and jealousy. As I grieved Alice's loss, I was finally able to realize that when these strong emotions came so close together and blended to create such a dramatic reaction, I missed a critical chance to stop and listen, surrender to God, and seize the opportunity to know and understand myself and my calling.

The dictionary says that *envy* means discontented longing for someone else's advantages, while *jealousy* means unpleasant suspicion or apprehension of rivalry. It adds that many people use the word jealousy to mean the same thing.[4] I am probably one of those many people. I always longed to be as beautiful as Alice and enjoy the advantages I imagined her beauty brought, and you've already read about my suspicions and sense of rivalry. Glennon Doyle says, "We're only envious of those already doing what we were made to do. Envy is a giant, flashing arrow pointing us toward our destiny."[5] I like this idea. Deep in my heart, it was never really about her physical beauty. Alice had a beautiful heart just like my mother's, and I don't believe she would ever have done anything to hurt me.

If my story of envy or jealousy has a flashing arrow, I pray that it points to a destiny involving beauty of the kind I most admire—inner beauty, a beautiful heart, the one I've given to God. What a glorious destiny to imagine and embrace!

After all these years, I finally have lost my distaste for having greenish eyes. It seems that just as tears are not all about sadness, jealousy is not always negative. Although I long associated jealousy with only darkness and sinfulness, God has taken me to His Word and shown me another side of it. In Exodus 20:5, we are told, "…for I the Lord your God am a jealous God." That is emphatic, but what do we make of it? In his devotional *You Are The Beloved*, Henry Nouwen tells of his longing for giving his whole life to God while at the same time feeling a sense of resistance to the possible loss of independence. This resistance called his attention to an important aspect of our relationship with God, and he uses his experience to assure us that God's extraordinary, divine love is, in fact, a jealous love. While this is nothing at all like the type of sinful jealousy that causes us to envy, suspect, and resent others, God does not just want part of us. He wants our surrendered selves—all our love and nothing less. Nouwen explains that this affirms God's abiding love for us. Only when we surrender ourselves completely to God's love can we be free from all the distractions, ready to actually hear the voice of divine love and recognize our own unique and precious call.[6]

THIRTEEN

Laughing and Crying

Emotions create the music of life while tears
reveal the changing melody.
—D. Cockerham

As true as the statement above is and considering the countless occasions for tears, it seems that the first mention of the word "tears" elicits a picture of sorrow, grief, melancholy, exhaustion, or gloom and doom. That is unfortunate because there are many varieties of lighthearted weeping: happy tears, sweet tears, laugh-until-you-cry tears, and cry-until-you-laugh tears.

No matter what variety, each tear has its own special mission. It is called into action by our finely tuned emotions, which have a delicate sense for difference. While your mind can instantly conjure happy tears, they are not different in color or shape from other tears. They don't run down your face in a different direction or give away any clues that they are to be recognized for their special meaning. How many emotions do tears represent? They are limitless, maybe … like the stars, someone said.

With every passing thought, a tear waits in the wings to be

called upon to put on a show. After all, that is really what tears are ... our show! They are our special gift for showing the world exactly how we feel. Too bad so few of us really understand tears. Even laughter and tears often embrace and together form a magical show of overwhelming joy. Now that's a show worth watching!

Sweet tears are not sweet to the taste. They actually taste pretty salty, like any other kind of tear. Like many tears, sweet tears accompany feelings. It's the feelings that are sweet. In fact, if you consider the definition of the word "sweet," it's not at all just about the taste, as in sweet tea and sweet potatoes. It also means satisfying, lovable, kind, pleasant, and even melodious.

Sweet tears are often present at ceremonies and holidays. Parents cry at their children's graduations and weddings. Almost everyone cries when the Budweiser Clydesdale horses gallop across the television screen through the snow pulling a red sleigh while snowflakes fall all around, holiday music plays in the background, and smoke circles the chimney outside of the lovely little houses. The velvety voice of the announcer plucks our heartstrings with warm words reminding us how delightfully sweet it is being home for the holidays. This rings true when considering the words of Kahlil Gibran in his poem "On Joy and Sorrow": "When you are joyous, look deep into your heart and you shall find it is only that which has given you sorrow that is giving you joy. When you are sorrowful, look again in your heart, and you shall see that in truth you are weeping for that which has been your delight."[1]

I often experience sweet tears. Not long ago, while reading Jan Karon's book *To Be Where You Are*,[2] I was moved by an exchange between the young father Dooley and his son Jack. Dooley was super busy and found himself being mean to Jack. This made Jack cry, and then his dad realized how selfish and unfeeling he had been to quickly respond, without thinking, in a hurtful way. Dooley was so moved that he began to cry too, and Karon explained that little Jack did not know that dads cried. As I pictured the young dad and his small son crying together and wiping each other's tears away, I reacted with tears of my own—sweet tears.

Although they both come from emotions that we take pleasure in, *sweet tears* are not the same as *happy tears*. Happy tears are all about being happy—over-the-top happy in a jumping-up-and-down, throwing confetti, and waving balloons type of way. It's when all of that is not even enough, and from deep inside our heart and soul come our own balloons, confetti, and fireworks, all in the form of a custom-made, personalized expression of supreme happiness: *happy tears*. As Leonardo da Vinci said, "Tears come from the heart and not from the brain." A friend recently shared a story about watching a favorite movie about dogs with her grandchild. They were cuddled up together on the sofa, eating popcorn and sharing giggles through the movie until, toward the end, the film moved my friend to sobs and heavy tears as the dog that had been lost was found. Her grandchild became frightened to see Grandma cry. My friend stumbled to explain, and through her tears, she realized that she needed to assure the child that she was okay and that her tears were *happy tears*.

As we experience life and grow from infants to toddlers and then preschoolers who only cry when unhappy or sad, when do we first experience happy tears? How do we react and how do we explain?

I remember my first happy tears as a young adult when my parents gave me a car as a gift. It was used and had a few dents but was exactly what I wanted and meant they really loved me. Perhaps, for many of us, it is that first stupendous gift that calls out happy tears for the first time ... tears that signify an extreme emotion of joy—unspeakable joy.

Laugh-until-you-cry tears are rather strange, primarily because they throw us off. We don't expect laughing and crying to go together, but it happens in endearing and long-remembered ways. As you know by now, I am a major weeper and rarely have control of my tears. When I start crying, much like when I start sneezing with my allergies, it just happens, and I have yet to find a way to gracefully hide what is clearly happening all over my face. I cannot remember when I began crying in ways that embarrassed me, but one of my first memories is from a Christmas many decades ago when I was engaged to Ralph. How that happened is the story you read about earlier, one full of mistakes and misguided decisions, and we ultimately broke up. But that Christmas, Ralph and I were together, and we were spending the holiday with my family in our big, comfy den near the glimmer of the Christmas tree lights and the warm glow of the fireplace. Gifts were everywhere, and when I unwrapped the large box with my name on it and saw what was inside, I felt breathless. Ralph had given me a stunning outfit ... I can almost remember every detail. The white cashmere sweater with pearl buttons and matching skirt were simply gorgeous. Glamorous and luxurious, the clothes were such an extravagant gift.

I was giddy with delight and so surprised that he had chosen something that lovely for me that I laughed out loud. When he hugged me, I began to cry and, as usual, it took a while for me to calm down. It was awkward, as it caught everyone off guard, and they looked the other way until I pulled myself together.

I believe that when emotions mix together like this, human nature kicks in and hints that something may be amiss. Underlying that particular weeping was a very insecure girl who was intimidated by a man she did not trust and wasn't even sure she loved. She loved the *idea* that someone so handsome (in her eyes) could love her, but the emotions that her insecurity aroused told the truth with her tears.

Dr. Oriana R. Aragón, a Yale University psychologist and assistant professor at Clemson University's College of Business, explains, "When individuals accomplish something, like winning a tennis championship or finishing a big race, they often feel overwhelming emotions." Aragón, who has completed numerous studies on the expression of emotions, goes on to say, "When those emotions become highly intense, they seem to manifest in physical expressions that, on the surface, look a little contrary to how one is actually feeling on the inside." She calls those expressions (when one cries because of overwhelming happiness) "dimorphous expressions."[3]

In his documentary *Laughing and Crying*, Mike Downie gives an inside look at the science behind laughter and crying, two of our earliest and most universal ways of communicating. He filmed everything from laughing babies in Vermont to super-criers in England to mule deer responding to their infants' cries. When interviewed, Downie reminisced about how the project roused memories of his own lifelong experiences with laughing and crying. He reflected that with this came the realization that laughing and crying are the soundtrack to life's most important and memorable moments.[4] I believe this is profoundly true and urge you to think back on the highs and lows in your own life. Consider what part crying and laughing have played in creating your soundtrack, your very own theme song—the music and changing melody of your life.

In closing, we need look no further than the Bible for more wisdom on laughing and crying. The writer of Ecclesiastes wrote, "To everything there is a season, and a time to every purpose under the heaven: A time to be born, and a time to die; a time to plant, and a time to pluck up that which is planted; A time to kill, and a time to heal; a time to break down, and a time to build up; A time to weep, and a time to laugh; a time to mourn, and a time to dance" (Ecclesiastes 3:1–4 KJV).

FOURTEEN
Tears of Deep Gratitude

Feeling gratitude and not expressing it is like wrapping a present and not giving it.
—**William Arthur Ward**

We have explored emotional tears that are connected to various experiences like repentance and jealousy. But what about tears of gratitude? Do we connect tears with a feeling of gratefulness and thankfulness, and are those the same as feelings of joy and happiness? Let's consider what it is like to be astounded with a feeling of appreciation, of being blessed, lucky, or utterly thankful. Have you experienced the sense of being completely free of any other thought or worry because this all-consuming emotion overrides everything else? We have all seen the examples of these moments, such as the videos of a child bawling uncontrollably when receiving a brand-new puppy or the mother sobbing inconsolably when her soldier son returns safely from Afghanistan.

Those moments embody gratitude—deep gratitude. How long does the moment last, and how do you acknowledge or pay tribute to that "grateful" feeling? What is sufficient? What, as humans, can we possibly do or say that rises to the heights of praise that adequately recognizes our utter gratitude? We find a clue in the word "gratitude," derived from the Latin word *gratus*. The Latin root word is grace. The Bible connects grace and gratitude in 1 Corinthians 1:4: "I give thanks to my God always for you because of the grace of God that has been given to you in Christ Jesus."[1] This brings back fond memories of growing up in a Christian home and sharing holidays with Christian friends and family. How touching that our prayer of thanks before a meal was called "Grace."

Amazingly, tears are our precious, personal, unique gifts of response to divine moments of grace. When we are extremely grateful, we experience a breathless, heart-stopping glimpse into our oneness with God. We fully appreciate his grace toward us. Through the lens of gratitude, we see the gift of life and our connection to our Creator.[2] Tears in these moments often take us by surprise and are somehow different from the experience of spiritual thankfulness and joy. They are similar, and certainly our lives with Christ and our study of the Bible have taken us on a precious journey full of emotional rejoicing as presented in Jeremiah 31:9: "Tears of joy will stream down their faces, and I will lead them home with great care. They will walk beside quiet streams and on smooth paths where they will not stumble."

Take a few minutes to remember times when you were astounded with gratitude. Roll back the years and slowly move through them until you find the moments when your entire being celebrated. Remember the spontaneous jumping up and down, the cheers of elation, the hugging, the kissing, the goose bumps, the euphoria, and the absolute delight spreading through every square inch of you. Did those actions satisfy your heart and soul's desire to reach out and embrace the giver of it all—or did you weep spontaneous, uncontrollable tears of gratitude?

I remember one such time. We had been praying for a friend's brother for months after he was diagnosed with a brain tumor. His sister knew he was an atheist, but as a devout Christian, she strongly believed in the power of prayer. Sharing his story and appealing for help with all she could muster, she pulled together an army of prayer warriors. I have no idea how large the army became, but through the months, she would faithfully send out updates to every member making sure we were aware of each scan, each chemo treatment, and each detail of her brother's struggles. If she knew of the tiniest encouraging sign of a breakthrough in his relationship with Christ, she would share it, but there were few signs of progress. That did not deter her. Her prayer warriors were not deterred. What held them together? What can friendship elicit that is so strong to bind together the hearts of people who don't even know each other? Is it our need to be connected? Is it faith or love? Or is it "gratitude in the making?"

Finally, the message came. After all the months and all the bad news, my friend's update read, "The most amazing news came from his wife. He said that he is willing to try to pray." Those words on that screen may as well have been golden, diamond, and sapphire-coated letters. They were so valuable, so rich in deep meaning and hope. Tears did not take more than one slight moment to burst forth like fireworks from my eyes in an explosion of pure and complete gratitude. Did the tears satisfy? Were they equal to the gift that was given with those words? I cannot imagine what else could have expressed my emotions more eloquently, more fervently, or more intimately. It brought to mind a quote by Thornton Wilder, who said, "We can only be said to be alive in those moments when our hearts are conscious of our treasures."[3] I felt fully alive in that moment, and with my tears came an assurance that God was listening to our army of prayer warriors—of course He was.

Months later, a few days before the man's death, when he could not speak, his wife talked to him again about Jesus and asked him to squeeze her hand if he believed and accepted Jesus as Lord of his life. He squeezed her hand. Praise God! Tears of joy and the acceptance of God's glorious presence in our lives came together, bringing deep, blessed peace.

Truly, coming face to face with God's grace leads to breathtaking, deep gratitude and uncontrollable, genuine tears of joy. These tears are messengers that come straight from our hearts, and God loves this genuine expression of our deep affection for Him. Yes, our tears are equal to the gift. Yes, they satisfy. Responding to God's grace spontaneously results in something magical, supernatural, mysterious, and wonderful. These tears are simple and yet so exquisite. They are our instinctive gift of gratitude to God.

> *"Gratitude is the sweetest thing in a seeker's life— in all human life. If there is gratitude in your heart, then there will be tremendous sweetness in your eyes."*
> **—Sri Chinmoy**[4]

FIFTEEN
Forgiving Yourself with Tears

Don't cry over spilled milk.
   —Benjamin Franklin

What's so bad about spilling the milk anyway? Is that what Ben Franklin meant? Surely some spilled milk is not worth crying about—bigger fish to fry and all that. What's a little puddle of milk? Maybe a mess. Maybe wasted food for the baby … or maybe something much worse. After all, milk means different things to different people.

When I hear the phrase "forgive and forget," I must admit I tend to shrug it off as something that comes easily to me. Sure, I have lived long enough to have had lots of opportunities to forgive. Admittedly, I haven't always forgiven right away, but eventually, I have forgiven even the lowest of blows and hurts and gone on my way.

However, this is when I am forgiving *others.* The real trick is when it comes to forgiving myself. I have decided that when you forgive others, you have made up your mind that they *do* deserve to be forgiven. If they spill the milk, it's okay, but not so much when I make a mess.

Now don't get me wrong—I may feel *worthy* enough to forgive myself and *do* completely understand that God forgives me for all the messes I make. I guess I just don't believe that I have the right to forgive myself, whether I'm worthy or not. It's not that my forgiveness is more valuable or sacred than God's forgiveness, it's just that I have made enough mistakes and spilled enough milk that I feel ashamed and seriously question whether forgiving myself can ever clean it all up.

By now you have probably figured out that spilled milk, messes, and sins all go together for me. All of these are mistakes. All of them need to be forgiven and forgotten, yet they linger, both the small messes and the big messes. I beat up on myself about them all. I am ashamed.

But what if crying could wash it all away? Is that why tears seem to hold a special power and why we tend to cry over spilled milk and messes, whether we think of them as mistakes or sins, in hopes that tears *will* wash the memory and the pain away? Could it be that tears are the link to forgiving ourselves? After all, we are the only creatures who shed emotional tears, and tears are our soul's connection to God. However, sometimes the tears we so desperately need to cry to release us from our shame stay bottled up inside, and forgiveness eludes us. I have suffered from this.

I carry memories of times I lost control that led me to a place of needing my own forgiveness. Once, when my son Jimmy was around five years old, this beautiful, blond, curly-haired little being vanished from the backyard where I had just seen him minutes before. I was instantly hot all over and heard a buzzing in my ears that was audible fear. All my instincts kicked in: I was a mother animal in a frenzy going in whatever direction seemed to lead to relief and imagining his sweet face smiling up at me and him saying, "Hi, Mommy." It was unlike any other fear … a fear to truly fear.

After thrashing all around the yard, I finally took a breath, stopped, and stood still. Breathing helped me think, and with that, I realized that he could not have gone far.

I walked to the front of the house and looked up and down the street, and when I turned to look back at our house, I saw movement next door. The movement was in the neighbor's backyard … little heads. I sprinted to that backyard. But instead of sheer joy and loving embraces, when I reached my son, I unleashed anger with screams and all the vengeance that a wild animal would use to grab up her baby and take it back to where it should be and where it was safe.

My tirade frightened everyone within shouting distance, but you can be assured that I did not care one bit, not one bit. I did not care what anyone else thought and did not even consider what Jimmy thought or how he felt. It did not matter—all that mattered was his precious hand in mine, coming with me, staying with me in safety.

This was not my best hour. Needless to say, Jimmy was so frightened that I am not sure he understood at all. From his perspective, he had been playing with his little friend Dawn; what was wrong with that? She lived right next door.

Did I cry with relief? Was I a hot mess after all of this? No. Sadly, no. It seems that feeling out of control can come on unexpectedly for me, and that frightens me. Oh, let me tell you, there are other stories of times I have behaved badly that are much worse. Times I struggle to forget. Sadly, instead of crying over the messes, sins, and "spilled milk" and forgiving myself and going on with life, I often harbor a heavy sense of guilt and deep disappointment in myself.

Now this is a long way to go to explain my difficulty with forgiving myself, but I want to help you see how it is connected to tears: *invisible tears*. These are tears I cry but no one sees. Mostly I cry with tears that are so terribly locked away that they do not show; they cannot rise to that level of escaping their deep well of pain. They languish there, causing me to cry with silent sobs and have bad dreams. These *invisible tears* seem to bring no relief and only drive the pain further and further into my core and into my soul where I feel ashamed, and it seems nothing can rescue me.

Tears, which God gave us to connect our souls to Him, need to well up and bring escape. But my tears are often stuck in a deep well. They are not welling *up*. They are deep *down* where the sins, messes, and spilled milk haunt me, where my failures become more and more awful and stand in the way of my forgiving myself.

Perhaps you share my weakness thinking that true forgiving is so powerful, so absolutely divine, that it is not ours to possess. The forgiving of myself is, after all, not the ultimate challenge. It's really about claiming God's promise. It's about lacking the *confidence* for forgiving myself. It's about being gentle with myself and letting His gift of tears, my connection with The Almighty, heal my suffering. According to the Bible, "If we confess our sins, he is faithful and just to forgive us our sins and to cleanse us from all unrighteousness" (1 John: 1:9 ESV).

After all, He has forgiven me. Jesus paid the price for my

spilled milk, my messes ... my sins. He wants me to feel confident to forgive and forget my sins and my mistakes and to forgive and forget my weaknesses. And, yes, with the power He has given me, I can cry the tears of rejoicing, the tears of true freedom and joy, knowing that He and I together can do all things—even dance our way right around all the spilled milk. As we read in Psalm 116:8, "For you have delivered my soul from death, my eyes from tears, my feet from stumbling."

Jimmy has gone on to be a successful professional with an adorable wife, Carmen, and two precious children named Noah and Carlee. In the meantime, I make mistakes and will continue to do so, and yet being unable to forgive myself is being afraid of all that God wants for me. That's right: It is a done deal. I am free to cry, free to forgive and forget, free to walk confidently with Him just as I am. As C. S. Lewis wrote in one of his letters, "If God forgives us, we must forgive ourselves. Otherwise, it's like setting up ourselves as a higher tribunal than Him."[1] Truth is, by not forgiving ourselves, we are playing God and turning our backs on Him, refusing His loving mercy and grace.

How could we possibly do that? Talk about spilled milk!

SIXTEEN
Second Chances

But this I call to mind, and therefore I have hope:
The steadfast love of the Lord never ceases; his
mercies never come to an end; they are new
every morning; great is your faithfulness.
—Lamentations 3:21–23

I've shared my experience with losing my son Jimmy in the neighborhood and the terrible fear that shattered my self-control. I am delighted to tell you a different version of much the same story—my second chance with my second son. However improbable it may seem to be, God gave me a second chance to get it right.

My husband Jim and I began skiing in Colorado when we first met. He had skied for several years, and after watching many movies featuring skiers having such exciting adventures in beautiful, snow-covered mountains, I loved the idea of learning to ski. The first year, I took lessons for five days straight. I have never fallen down so many times, going in so many different directions and laughing until I cried. The pain was such a small price to pay for the fun, the excitement, and the sheer joy of learning something that brought such delight.

Gliding through space with the beautiful Rocky Mountains all around me, with snow on my hair and eyelashes and a song in my heart—what could be more heavenly? I fell in love with it. Skiing became an annual event, and even after our babies were born, we somehow managed to never miss our Colorado ski trip. As soon as we decided that the boys were old enough, they went along with us.

I never would have believed that I could adore everything about skiing any more than I already did, but I was wrong. Watching my boys in bright ski outfits on their little skis, bouncing along with their bottoms barely above the snow, laughing and loving it—well, that was the icing on the cake!

Jim's sister Jane was a skiing enthusiast and joined us for at least two of our trips. She was along on the vacation that gave me my second chance. We had decided that although Jeff was only four years old, he was ready to ski, and Jane could help if needed. We signed him up for ski school (I use that term loosely since at his age it was more like babysitting), and I bought new outfits just for him (none of his brother's hand-me-downs would do). He was over-the-moon excited and we all could hardly wait to be together in God's beautiful Rocky Mountains.

Traveling always takes coordination, and for a ski trip, you have the added hassle of equipment rental, ski school registration, and last-minute shopping when you discover the weather is warmer than usual or, conversely, when a blizzard arrives. All of this was part of our first day and set the stage for the dramatic, never-to-be-forgotten incident with Jeff.

Jeff is a handsome guy and, back then, he was about as cute as they come. He had curly, dark-brown hair and big brown eyes and almost always wore a smile on his face. He was a little shy but generally confident about taking on any new adventure.

We had just checked into our big, beautiful suite of rooms in a Breckenridge, Colorado, high-rise hotel and were unpacking, changing clothes, and figuring out how the television worked. In other words, we were completely absorbed with getting settled before heading out to walk in the snow, shop a little, and enjoy dinner that night at one of the mountainside restaurants. I am not sure how long this went on before I moved on to find Jimmy and Jeff and make sure they were all set. Jimmy had started a puzzle with Jane in front of the big fireplace in the main room, but where was Jeff? That's right—we could not find him anywhere.

At first, we thought he was playing hide and seek. Remember, at the time, he was only four. But we soon realized that he was gone. "Gone" is never a good word, but it is especially bad when it applies to your child. Panic, fear, and a hurried pace ensued big time! However, my second chance kicked in. After shaking all over and praying the fastest prayer I'd ever uttered, I pulled myself together and, along with Jim, led the way to quickly execute a plan for finding Jeff with no delay. I called the front desk while Jim went out the front door and down the hall to the left; Jane and Jimmy went down the hall to the right. But what about the elevator and all the other floors? That's where the front desk came in, and I was putting together a plan with the hotel concierge service when Jeff appeared. He stood in front of me with that beautiful, mischievous smile and said, "Hi, Mom. I'm back." He was so pleased with his fine adventure and the two lovely teenage girls who'd found him wandering down the hall. He had no idea how close he had come to being lost, being gone—really gone.

It seems that while we were executing our carefully conceived "seek and rescue mission," Jeff was happily finding his way along the super-long hallway, looking in every open door, saying hello to anyone he met (it was check-in time so lots of folks were arriving), and generally loving the freedom of the unknown. He was intrigued by the elevator and probably planned to jump on it when the doors opened right in front of him. But when those two precious teen angels stepped out of the elevator, they realized he was alone and scooped him up. They knew right away that he needed the safety they could provide, and they decided to help him find his family. The girls started right near the elevator and knocked on each door looking for people Jeff would recognize. These two girls were not about to let anyone near their new friend unless they were totally sure that he was in the right place with the right people. Once they found us, they told us how they had fallen in love with Jeff immediately.

Angels are everywhere and come in all different shapes, sizes, ages, and outfits. They are often hard to recognize, especially at first. But in this case, as with a faded rainbow, I could barely see those girls' halos glowing. God works in such magical ways. I got my beloved Jeff back safe and sound, and I got a second chance at not losing control at a critical time. Above all, I got another reminder of how much God loves us. He loves me and really cares for me. Yes, of course, I cried. I cried tears of relief and supreme gratitude. Tears, my sweet tears, show up to highlight and enhance the important moments like that one and even some not-so-important moments. Tears are truly so much a part of who we are.

That ski trip turned out to be one that will always stand out from the rest for many reasons. To this day, Jeff, like the rest of us, loves skiing, but on that first trip, he thought it was awful! He wanted to ski with his big brother and could not understand why he had to stay in the stuffy building with lots of "little kids" and only ski down a tiny "baby hill" over and over. After all, how could that possibly compare with his first day's "big boy" adventure?

He's a young adult now with a beautiful wife (Rachel) and daughter (Stella Grace). With giant smiles and a lust for life, they have just headed off on their second year-long sailing adventure with their dog, Gus. Jeff never lost his adventurous spirit and, God knows, I pray every adventure will always include sweet angels with halos watching over him and his family in every way.

SEVENTEEN

Imagination: Clowns, Dolls, and Grown-up Tears

Imagination is everything. It is the preview of life's coming attractions.
—Albert Einstein

When I was little and we got our first television set in the early 1950s, my world expanded and stretched beyond our three-bedroom house and little yard to a magic world of wide-open spaces and places I'd never seen. The wonders of make-believe came to life. One of my very favorite shows was *Winky Dink and You*. My mother mailed in a check to buy me a Winky Dink kit. I would stick the magic plastic screen on the television during each show. With that screen and the special pens that came in my kit, I was an official "Winky Dink Helper" and could draw a bridge to help Winky get across the river or come to his rescue drawing in lots of different ways. It was one adventure after another each week and a complete delight. Who would have thought that *interactive technology* existed back in those early days of television? Well, it did, and I loved my life as a Winky Dink Helper. As the minister Norman Vincent Peale said, "Imagination is the true magic carpet."[1]

As much as I loved Winky Dink, the television show that I never wanted to miss—the absolute best television show that topped *Winky Dink* by far—was *The Howdy Doody Show*. Buffalo Bob Smith was the human star, but the magic face and voice that every kid loved was Howdy Doody, the beloved puppet. Howdy Doody and Buffalo Bob shared wonderful adventures each week and introduced kids to enchanting characters like Princess Summerfall Winterspring, Flub-a-dub, and Clarabell the Clown. Clarabell was special. He never spoke. Instead, he had a little horn with a rubber ball that he honked and honked.

Clarabell was my favorite character. He was always happy with his giant, painted-on smiley face and his bright, cheery yellow-and-red costume. He made me laugh when he danced and frolicked and made me sad when he rested his head on Buffalo Bob's shoulder to shed giant tears when things didn't go well. Howdy Doody always saved the day, and Clarabell would dance and honk his little horn with glee. It was giggles and such fun.

However, dolls were my first love. Before we had a television, and even later when I wasn't watching television, my favorite characters and friends were my dolls. I had paper dolls that I would cut out clothes for, and I had dolls like the one Santa Claus left under the tree for me. I named her Gloria after the beautiful lady next door. My make-believe world came to life as I filled hour after hour with pretending. Like fairy dust and twinkling fireflies, my world was nothing short of Peter Pan, Cinderella, and Snow White all wrapped up in my imagination. In the words of Helen Keller, "The most beautiful world is always entered through imagination."[2]

When I close my eyes and float back to that time, to those magical days of dolls and clowns and simple pleasures, I know love. You see, little children can learn love through the eyes of a puppet, the eyes of a clown, or the eyes of their puppy or kitty cat. God makes us in His image right from the start. He finds so many amazing ways to show us love and teach us about love. We don't even know what to call it much of the time, but we know it, we feel it, and we long for it. We are made for it, and with all of our senses, we recognize love.

Sadly, through the years, Hollywood has turned clowns into bad guys who hurt people. Films depict dolls as spooky characters living in attics waiting for some unsuspecting victim to come along so they can devour them or transform them into a zombie. The memories, joys, and love that were mine from these playthings has been stomped on, banished, and blotted out by these warped, ugly versions of my dear childhood friends. What remains is a wisp of wonder, a fleeting memory, a sweet and enchanting bygone moment.

In the same way, for many humans, God has become a "bad guy." Children and adults have turned away from God because His name has been used to frighten or belittle them. People have suffered ugly things done in the name of God and religion, or they have witnessed horrible things that have been so brutal, so harmful, and so awful that God's name has been defamed.

Is that what growing up is all about? Are grown-up tears the tears of a vague disappointment, the tears of loss, the tears of grief as we watch Peter Pan fly away forevermore? I don't believe it's the loss of our youth we suffer; I believe it's the loss of love. It's the loss of our first taste of love in the God-given, supernatural world of our childhood imagination, where images of wonder, images of delight, images of love, and images of God abound. Unfortunately, God has been misrepresented by so many people in ways that distort who He really is. The absolute truth is found in John 4:8: "God is Love." All the deep longing for something lost that you have known in your heart since you left your mother's womb—that is God.

The truth is, growing up can be a flop! But that is not the end of the story. In fact, it is just the beginning. For with that first taste of love comes the lifelong quest to find it again. Never forget that Jesus charged all of us to be more like children in our approach to faith and indeed to love: "Suffer little children, and forbid them not, to come unto me: for of such is the kingdom of heaven" (Matthew 19:14 KJV). He wants us to love, trust, and imagine like children.

That is the key to the kingdom of heaven. That is the key to connecting with God. You see, our ultimate destination is the Kingdom of God. There in God's presence, when you do find love again in all its wonder, magic, and light, the Divine in all of us will kiss you on the cheek and say, "I've been right here through it all, loving you every step of the way."

EIGHTEEN

Creativity and Emotions

*Rational thoughts never drive people's creativity
the way emotions do.*
   —Neil deGrasse Tyson

Creativity and good, healthy crying go hand in hand to prolong our youth and remind us that we truly have a supernatural source. In an article about the surprising benefits of crying, Daniel Wallen says that crying is extraordinarily good for the creative process. He goes on to say that creativity stirs the imagination, gets the juices flowing, and makes us feel alive in new and exciting ways.[1]

When considering creativity, it's worth repeating that the first recorded emotion that God expressed in the Bible was when He stepped back from His creation and saw that it was *good*. The first chapter of Genesis declares "God saw that it was good" after each day of creation (verses 4, 10, 12, 18, 21, 25). On the sixth day, with the creation of humans, God saw that it was "very good" (Genesis 1:31). He had feelings. He expressed delight. We know that Jesus, the Son of God, wept (John 11:35), and I can imagine that God wept right there in the very beginning—wept with unspeakable joy and pure delight!

Creativity is a natural human process. Wallen asserts that whether you are a writer, filmmaker, dancer, or even a fledgling artist, crying is a necessary practice to comprehend and feel what you're making.[2] And if you do not feel it, neither will anyone else. As poet Robert Frost said, "No tears in the writer, no tears in the reader. No surprise for the writer, no surprise for the reader."[3] It is true that if the results of your creative works are not powerful for you, they will not be powerful for your audience. Even when we know it is an actor delivering a crucial line in a play, his rousing, powerful delivery can certainly make it believable and bring us to tears. How about that stirring, powerful chorus in the opera when many of us do not understand Italian and have absolutely no idea what words are being sung—and yet we weep?

Yes, in these moments, we are left with such a healthy, lovely sense of the sublime that is reminiscent of Julia Roberts's tears during her evening at the opera in *Pretty Woman*.[3] That scene and her tears touched our collective hearts. Her vulnerability was endearing and such a pleasant reminder of the supernatural source we all share. No matter who we are, God loves our tears and rejoices when our souls respond to creativity or creation.

As a child, my favorite thing about school was being the "teacher's helper" for each of my elementary teachers, except my first-grade teacher who put me in the corner with a dunce cap for crying and wanting to go home (but that's another story). I gloried in having a chance to clean up the room, sharpen pencils, wipe down the chalkboard, and do just about anything my teachers asked. They were always so pleased with me, and their glowing comments filled me with joy and such a wonderful sense of being important in some small way. The truly best part, though, was when they asked me to help with a teaching aid project. This always involved being creative. I would build a papier-mâché volcano, paint a large picture of a clown to hang on the door, or even neatly print messages for the next day's lessons on the blackboard. Walking home from school after these afternoons of being the helper were special times for skipping, singing, and happy tears as I let myself feel the keen emotion of unspeakable joy.

Junior high school held little chance to be the teacher's helper, and I struggled along trying to find my creative niche. My wonderful parents knew how important it was for me to be creative and supported me with every effort. I took dance lessons but was ashamed of my slip-ups and quit. I played clarinet in the band until I grew frustrated at having to march in a wool uniform and heavy hat in eighty-nine-degree weather. With no lessons at all, I still had determined audacity and tried out for cheerleader and bombed out—several times. These were my first real experiences with disappointment and failure, and with each failed attempt at being creative came tears—tears of frustration and sorrow. I hid them, tried to have a "stiff upper lip," and moved further and further away from being "teacher's helper" and the creative bliss I had enjoyed when life was easier and more fun. I agree with Pablo Picasso, who is said to have remarked that every child is an artist, but the real trick is remaining an artist as you grow up.

My own experiences show that as I grew, I became less inclined to try things, to be creative, to step outside the box. Research shows I'm not the only one. Sir Ken Robinson was a

British educator, writer, and expert on creativity who advocated for the incorporation of art classes into school curriculums. He was an amazing orator—his three TED talks have been viewed an astounding 21.5 million times. In them, he stated that schools with traditional educational approaches kill emotions and creative abilities. His research showed that 90 percent of preschool children present high levels of creative thinking. After years at school, barely 20 percent of the same children at age twelve have maintained those levels of what he calls "divergent thinking."[4]

When it comes to being creative, kids, unlike adults, will take a chance. Robinson cautioned that if you are not willing to be wrong, you will struggle to come up with anything original. He continued by declaring that children are not frightened of being wrong—if they don't know, they will "have a go."[5] Adults lose that capacity. They become frightened of making mistakes. Yet we run our schools and companies in a way that stifles creativity. Robinson's popular message was based on his belief that kids lose their willingness to make mistakes by the stigmatization of being wrong. I agree. In addition, I believe that demeaning and belittling our children's tears fits right in with "being wrong."

Even if you don't work in the arts and are not a famous performer or designer of some sort, every job is creative in some way. Creativity is becoming more and more of a requirement in the twenty-first century, not just for the arts but for industry, science, and technology. Along with the recognition of the value of creativity has come evidence that an individual's emotional characteristics have an explicit impact on their artistic and creative abilities. In recognition of this trend, Scott

Kaufman, scientific director of the Imagination Institute at the University of Pennsylvania, in an article for *Harvard Business Review*, discusses emotions that make us more creative. He cites several studies affirming that living life with passion and intensity is conducive to creativity.[6]

Crying is a form of being intensely emotional that many creative people share. Interviews with talented actors and other artists often uncover how many of them talk about crying as almost a facet of their personality. For example, actress Jessica Chastain says that she is extremely sensitive in real life and will inevitably cry if someone around her is crying. She calls it her weakness or sensitivity.[7] Likewise, Taylor Swift confesses that when you walk out on a stage in front of thousands of people, it can bring you to tears.[8]

Going back to Sir Ken Robinson for a moment, let's consider one of his seminal quotes: "All children start their school careers with sparkling imaginations, fertile minds, and a willingness to take risks with what they think."[9]

Now, doesn't it give you goose bumps to imagine rediscovering and unleashing that child hiding inside each of us? That child is yearning to break through the barriers to "have a go," to dance, to cry, to create all the beautiful things that only God knows are still yet to be ours.

> *"There is a Fountain of Youth: it is your mind, the talents, the creativity you bring to your life and lives of the people you love. When you learn to tap this source, you will truly have defeated age."*
> **—Sophia Loren**[10]

NINETEEN

Achieving Balance

Wisdom is your perspective on life, your sense of balance, your understanding of how the various parts and principles apply and relate to each other.

—Steven R. Covey

Throughout my adult life, I've been impressed by the recurring message that echoes the wisdom in seeking balance—steadiness, poise, and stability in all that we do. My first experience with having balance was in fifth grade when I was assigned the role of "tightrope walker" for our school's Halloween Festival. This was a big deal. All the students and families attended the festival along with the teachers, the principals, and friends from other schools. I went straight to my daddy for ideas and wound up with a balance beam that he constructed using big concrete blocks and long two-by-four boards. Two or three sections were one-and-a-half feet off the floor.

With my arms held high out at my sides and my toes pointed like a circus performer, I nimbly navigated this imaginary tightrope wearing my pretty pink ballet slippers, a tutu from my dance class, and even makeup with rosy cheeks and lipstick. I did this again and again, all night long. It was awesome fun, but it was not easy. With friends and family looking on, I would get distracted and fall. A few friends snickered, but it sure wasn't funny to me. A couple of times I tried to show off and do a few little jumps. That was a disaster. But after tears from embarrassment and a bloody skinned knee that had to be covered with a Band-Aid, I was back up on my tightrope entertaining the crowds.

When it comes to balance, William Arthur Ward's words seem to go especially well with this little story: "A well-developed sense of humor is the pole that adds balance to your steps as you walk the tightrope of life."[1]

Keeping our balance is the key to so much of what we encounter in life. But maintaining our equilibrium is not easy. With every endeavor comes a different set of things to balance while navigating what is often a narrow path to success. And there are distractions.

One of the areas of life that requires clear vision and a keen sense of balance actually affects everything we do. That's the counterbalance of our hearts and our minds. Tears from our hearts can often blur our vision. That's where our heads come in to adjust the lens and provide balance. Emotions, feelings, opinions, and beliefs guide us from our hearts. Reason, intelligence, logic, and good sense direct us from our heads. But how do emotions and tears combine with logical reasoning to achieve a balanced outcome? Is it conceivable that this could be accomplished in all aspects of our lives? I'm not sure, but I know for myself that it can certainly happen.

Choices happen every day. Some are small and rather insignificant, and others go on framing our lives for years to come. Such was the heart and head choice I made when my world fell apart and my life changed completely.

My husband and I were going in different directions and marriage was gradually becoming a difficult part of life. Jim and I tried to hold it together. We faced so many questions, with one of the most important ones being if we should stay together for our children. The boys were fourteen and nine at the time. We sought answers by consulting with counselors, taking trips to have together time, and talking and talking. I cried, got angry, smoked cigarettes, and drank wine, but nothing worked. We finally did choose to divorce and go our separate ways.

Meanwhile, my job at the hospital was about to be discontinued, and the new job offer meant moving away. It could offer a fresh start perhaps, but I would be away from the city I loved and my children. Of course, I had no plans to go off and leave them. That could never happen! But ultimately, that is exactly what I did. How could a mother do that? With eerie memories of movies about heart-wrenching choices parents must make, I mustered all my courage, swallowed my pride, and surrendered to the guidance of the child psychologists, ministers, marriage counselors, and other experts who said boys should be with their dad. I was told that they were both at such a fragile and critical age in their development that being with their male parent, who was a good person, would be best.

For months, I drove seventy-six miles from Charlotte to Spartanburg throughout the week and every weekend to spend time with my sons. For years, I took them with me on every business trip and invented ways that we could be together. I did my best to make the most of it, but it was the most difficult decision I ever made. And yet, it is one that I do not regret. They grew to be fine men, wonderful husbands, fathers, and sons. Jim was a good dad and God was there every minute through it all. Yes, I second-guess myself to this day and am uncomfortable about what others might think of that decision. Yes, I still don't know if the boys understood or ever will, but while my heart screamed with anguish to have them with me, my head said, *you must do this.* Combining my deep love (my heart) with my extreme desire to do the right thing (my head), gave me balance and, ultimately, peace of mind. Trevor Hudson, in his book *The Serenity Prayer,* reminds us that not only has God repeatedly promised to forgive us and allow us to start again with a clean slate, but He has also promised to help us restore our broken and shattered lives to something of the usefulness and fullness they had before.[2]

As I mentioned, I spent some of the best years of my life raising my two sons in Spartanburg, South Carolina. One of the favorite sons of that fair city is former US Congressman Trey Gowdy. When discussing the art of persuasion in his book *Doesn't Hurt to Ask,*[3] Gowdy shares a touching account of his experience with a balanced heart and head approach to an important case he encountered while serving as solicitor for two counties in the Upstate area.

Gowdy faced a disturbing case involving an assistant principal whom he thought had been wrongfully accused of harming a child. The case had already been tried before a jury and ended in a mistrial when the jurors could not agree on a verdict. Gowdy, who would not normally get involved at this level, reviewed the case in response to an impassioned appeal from the principal who insisted that her assistant principal was innocent and that even a mistrial was a flagrant injustice. Remarkably, Gowdy decided to take the case back to court. He explains that when he met the defendant, he had no doubt that she was innocent. He describes her as being precisely the kind of person you would select to teach your own child or grandchild. She was caring, mild-mannered, gentle, and a person who looked for and believed the best of others.[4]

He relates that the assistant principal cried right in court—and so did Gowdy. She cried because she had been accused of the most sinister and harmful thing an educator can be accused of—hurting a child. Gowdy cried because he had witnessed a purity of spirit rarely seen and believed that truth would win out and the right thing would be done.[5] The right thing was done—she was acquitted.

I believe that this story effectively demonstrates that one of the keys to a balanced heart and head is often to go deep into your feelings and connect them to a larger principle or fundamental belief. To simply be "emotional" depreciates the value of emotions. To be effective, emotions should not be engineered. They must be authentic. Gowdy asserts that when we are emotional about a larger belief or truth, our emotions take on a quality of deep sincerity. Earnest emotions reflect heart and head reasoning.[6]

My experience involved my heart's deep emotional love for my children along with my own larger belief that their well-being and future were *the* fundamental truth and essence of being a mother—their mother.

In considering a quest for balance as a result of connecting emotions with a larger belief or truth, it is important to point out that through the centuries, eminent scholars have maintained that the soul actually has three essential elements. Most notably, Plato's *Theory of Soul* teaches that the soul's three parts are the mind/reason, the will/spirit, and the emotion/appetite. The spirit is identified with fearlessness, valor, and warrior-like qualities. The emotion/appetite is identified with desires such as greed, economic gains, physical comforts, and sensuous pleasures. Plato asserted that the highest faculty of the soul is the mind/reason, which is simple and indivisible, eternal, and immortal. The reason is beyond time and space, whereas spirit and appetite are within time and space. According to Plato, the reason is immortal and divine, while spirit and appetite are mortal and mundane.[7]

Theologians struggle with the question of whether a man is made up of two parts (namely body and soul/spirit) or three parts (body, soul, and spirit). Billy Graham explained that Christian psychologists and teachers popularized the concept of three parts because it provided a practical way to distinguish between man's material nature, his psychological being, and his spiritual relationship with God.[8]

Additionally, in his article "The Soul Having Three Parts," Witness Lee discusses Biblical evidence that the soul does indeed have three parts: the mind, the will, and the emotion.[9] He cites Proverbs 2:10 as spiritual evidence to substantiate that the mind is part of the soul: "For wisdom will enter your heart, and knowledge will be pleasant to your soul." Along with this reference to knowledge being a feature of the mind, Lee points to other Biblical references that indicate that knowledge is related to the soul.[10] He concludes that these verses make it clear that the mind, as the organ to know, to consider, and to remember, is a part of the soul.[11]

If we value these teachings, we have strong reason to affirm that our souls have all the elements needed for heart and head balance: mind/reason that represents our beliefs and our personal truths, along with our emotion/appetite that expresses our desires. Even as a little girl, I understood high up on my makeshift balance beam that balance was difficult to achieve. Yes, it is difficult, but it is not impossible. By applying our entire souls, we can achieve a balance that does not diminish the value of our emotions and includes our mind/reason as well as our spirit/will. We can all joyfully celebrate God with the Psalmist: "I praise you because I am fearfully and wonderfully made; your works are wonderful. I know that full well" (Psalm 139:14).

TWENTY

Hugs, Kisses, or Tears?

Life is our greatest possession and love its greatest affirmation.
—Leo F. Buscaglia

All five of our kids and grandkids carried their bags, jackets, and computers to the door, gave their hugs, and said their goodbyes. They then piled in their cars, waved really big, and drove away … never pausing for a moment in the whirlwind to say, "I love you." My husband and I teared up as their cars disappeared from view, and we slowly walked back into the house. We had said we loved them several times as they prepared to leave, but it just didn't seem to matter. They hadn't said it back.

Why bother saying "I love you" when it is so painful not to get a response? I know my kids and grandkids reciprocate our love. And my memory reminds me that I acted just the same when I was a young adult going in fifteen directions at once. I rarely took the time to express my emotions, even to the people I loved most.

I recognize now that I need to express and share my emotions, and I long for others to do the same. We yearn for people to demonstrate their love through hugs, kisses, saying "I love you," and perhaps even through tears. So, what is essential and crucial when it comes to expressing the emotion of love? And what is the ultimate expression of love?

A hug can go a long way for many people, and during the recent pandemic, we all came to better understand the value of hugs. In his book *The Vanishing Man*, Charles Finch describes the hug that only a mother can give—when part of her love passes into another person with a press of the body, holding in its few seconds all the history of sweet tenderness that harkens back to the time when mother and child were one.[1]

When it comes to thoughts of hugs and love, Leo Buscaglia's books have a special place on my bookshelf and in my heart. They are all about love. When he wrote his first book titled *LOVE*, he was surprised to find that the simple title *LOVE* had never previously been claimed, allowing him to say, "I have the copyright on LOVE!" He studied and wrote about pure, unadorned love—hugs for everyone—and the study of love brought him to the study of life. He believed and taught that to live in love is to live in life and to live in life is to live in love. But he would strongly assert that this should never be done passively. He stressed that we should each decide to live *for* something and create joy for others by sharing what we have and bringing hope to the lost and love to the lonely.[2]

Buscaglia's message resonated with millions. Before his death in 1998, he was best known for his many presentations on PBS, where his heartfelt talks became the largest single money generator for public broadcasting through much of the 1980s. I believe that the essence of his popularity was about our need as humans to express *and share* our emotions. We need each other. Tears, actions (like hugs and kisses), and loving words are about sharing, showing, living out, connecting, demonstrating, doing, being, and expressing love. God does that very thing over and over in each of our lives with every single breath, blink of the eye, and precious teardrop.

What about a kiss? A kiss is said to be a sensual act that expresses our love, emotions, and care without the need for any words. In many ways, a kiss goes beyond words by expressing feelings that may be difficult to say. It is the symbol of love, affection, and care. According to the internet, there are at least twenty different types of kisses. These include the forehead kiss, which is a gentle expression of admiration; a kiss on the hand that shows both admiration and passion; the affectionate Eskimo kiss, often given from a parent to their child; the French kiss; the earlobe kiss; the cheek kiss; the air kiss; and the ever-popular lingering kiss.

Each kiss symbolizes love in a different way and at a different level, which makes kissing amazingly versatile. Like tears, kisses have many different meanings and communicate varied messages. When put together, they harmonize and amplify the message.

Hugs and kisses convey so much, but I still prefer the three little words *I love you.* I love to dance, whether it is in the kitchen when no one is watching, or at a lovely wedding reception when my husband and I magically harken back to our days of bopping, doing the twist, or cuddling close for the slow tunes. But second only to actually "shaking a leg" comes watching an old Fred Astaire movie—sublime, beautiful elegance in motion. Astaire had lots of wonderful partners: Ginger Rogers, Cyd Charisse, Jane Powell, Leslie Caron, Audrey Hepburn, and Vera-Ellen. In the 1950 musical *Three Little Words*, Astaire and Vera-Ellen are perfection on the dance floor in the tuxedoed duet, "Where Did You Get That Girl?" But the best moment is a tender, romantic adagio called "Thinking of You." The musical numbers, including the title song, "Three Little Words," speak for themselves. The film was a huge hit. The public connected with the theme, and Fred Astaire won the very first Golden Globe award for best actor.[3]

The words "I love you," when exchanged, mean two people share the same feelings for each other. It's one thing to fall in love or be in love, but it's an entirely different matter if you are there all by yourself. Waiting, yearning, hoping, and praying for the words from the object of your affection that affirm you are not alone in how you feel can seem like an eternity. When they come, whether it's from your romantic dancing partner or your kids and grandkids, the stars fall from the skies, the air smells sweet, birds sing, and your world just goes into orbit at a magnificent new level. It is more than good. It is sensational!

Saying "I love you" and showing His love is what God does throughout the Bible and in every moment of our lives. He knows our deep need for Him and He yearns to share His expressions of love. Romans 8:32 assures us: "He who did not spare his own Son, but gave him up for us all—how will he not also, along with him, graciously give us all things?"

Certainly, love and tears go together. Who has known love and not wept at every turn in the winding road that love brings? There is certainly a difference in romantic love and familial love, but when it comes to tears, my life and the lives of my children and grandchildren started with tears, and I've never stopped crying for them as they experience the ups and downs of life. When my kids were babies, I held them, cuddled them, and wiped away their tears. In this way, I bonded with them. This is true with friends as well. Tears are a magic glue that ties us together. Think about the people you have cried with or cried about throughout your life. No matter the reason for the tears, all of those people more than likely have a special place in your heart that was sealed by tears.

In discussing the various qualities of tears in her study of emotions and tears, Dr. Karyn Hall points to several factors that give tears an edge over any other indicator of love. First, she says that tears send a signal of vulnerability and willingness to cooperate. She maintains that tears deter aggressive actions because they signal that you don't want conflict, and she stresses that in our modern society, fighting is not the most desired social skill. Instead, cooperation and a willingness to be vulnerable in relationships help build a life of contentment.[4]

Hall also discusses the very human reaction of crying in empathy when watching someone else cry. She suggests that allowing tears means the walls are down and the person is undefended. She elaborates by saying that this shedding of resistance is an opportunity for intimacy. Since tears are difficult to fake, they are often a sign of honesty to others.[5]

When contemplating an expression of love, it's hard to deny that in any kind of relationship, tears may often show trust. Our willingness to cry with someone and be comforted by the other person reveals a feeling of safety. It can build a fervent closeness, like the experience shared when a couple cries at their wedding or when their baby is born.

Tears seem to signal a powerful connection between thought and emotion, a way of expressing feelings that cannot be expressed in any other way. Some people may be uncomfortable with the intensity of the emotion expressed by tears or with the passion of the emotion aroused in them. The cause of their resistance could be that they are not comfortable with the vulnerability shown by someone who is crying.

Tears may very well be the ultimate expression of love. In any case, they do transcend the notions of romance, friendship, or family connection and are from the heart. The emotion of love reaches out in all directions, and tears may be the most important road signs along our journey—whatever the direction.

We've explored hugs, kisses, the three little words, and tears. When all of these expressions of love come together, we have an amazing experience. However, it all pales when compared to Divine Love—the love that passes all understanding. The love like no other love. We found it, and it found us —the ultimate expression of love. The Love of God is frequently mentioned in the Bible through stories and proverbs as divine, true, and everlasting. In fact, the Bible says that God *is* love! God's love far surpasses our human attempts at expressing love through gestures and words. God's expression of love, the ultimate expression of love, was the gift of His son Jesus Christ.

The Bible tells us, "For God so loved the world that he gave his one and only Son, that whoever believes in him shall not perish but have eternal life" (John 3:16). This Biblical theme continues with the verse, "Dear friends, let us love one another, for love comes from God. Everyone who loves has been born of God and knows God. Whoever does not love does not know God, because God is love" (John 4:7).

In wrapping up our search for the ultimate expression of love, C. S. Lewis says it all: "Though our feelings come and go, God's love for us does not."[6]

TWENTY-ONE

When the Crying Stops

Time engraves our faces with all the tears we have not shed.
—Natalie Clifford Barney

I have always been secretly proud of being the oldest of five children. Somehow it makes me feel worthy to have been given the blessing of sharing the cherished details of day-to-day life with all those lovely little souls.

For the longest time, it seemed that our family was destined to be just like the characters in Louisa May Alcott's book *Little Women*.[1] Daddy loved calling me and my sisters his little women. Every year on Valentine's Day, he gave us each a giant, heart-shaped red box with every imaginable flavor and shape of delicious chocolate candy inside. Each box was wrapped with a beautiful, red satin ribbon and personally addressed to each one of his four little women. I can see the gift tag now in my imagination with his distinct handwriting and the words: "To Diann—my little woman. Love, Daddy." Such a happy memory.

It was not a secret, however, that Daddy wished for a son. He was a sportsman who loved fishing, hunting with his bird dog, Sandy, and frog gigging when he had the chance. Although my sisters and I tried shooting guns and wading in the muck, we were girls, for goodness' sake. We never really got too good at being part of his rugged pastimes, but we certainly tried.

By the time my youngest sister came along, Mother and Daddy decided it best to accept the joy of four girls and put a final "exclamation point" on the having-kids thing by naming their last daughter Jimmie after my Daddy, James Gordon. That choice of punctuation, however, should have been a question mark. My brother, Cal, was born seven years later. When you've had three sisters and little hope of ever getting the brother you prayed for, that brother becomes even more special.

Cal and I were as close as a brother and sister can be when sixteen years separate them. I genuinely loved him deeply. It's just that he did not live long enough. When he was 24 years old, he took his own life. I did not weep. I've talked about invisible tears, and I know them personally. When we lost Cal, I had no tears. This is, in fact, another reason why tears and eyes are so sacred to me. I've shared throughout this book the significant role tears have played in my life. It is extremely difficult to put into words the kind of connection tears have to my emotions. And it's why it was so significant when I entered a time of deep emotion—having lost a cherished sibling—and found I could not cry.

Tears, like rain that falls from the clouds to grow our crops, fill our lakes, and clear the air, are a vital, divine source of renewal. When there is no rain, there is no calm after the storm. In the same way, without tears, there was no calm after my storm. The storm just raged on and on for years. I hid it deep within. I would not, could not, admit to myself that his suicide had actually happened. It was very much like total denial. Now, I know that there are stages of grief and mourning, but I never left the first stage. In fact, I never *entered* the first stage. It was as if my emotions, both my heart and my head, refused—they absolutely refused— to cooperate. I faced an incomprehensible reality, one that tears would not dispel. How do you cope with your brother taking his own life?

I wrote earlier about the uneasiness of being with someone who does not cry when every single bit of evidence confirms that tears are absolutely needed. I have been there, and to this day—to this day—it is as if I am someone else when it comes to accepting my brother's death. I've introduced myself to you as the weeper, the emotional lover of all things that touch the heart and soul. But that someone did not make an appearance in the chapter of my life when my brother died.

I believe that "emotions create the music of life while tears reveal the changing melody." How, then, do I explain this absence of my tears, which are the very essence of my soul's melody?

It's such a void—this absence of tears and words. But tragically, the actual void, the actual absence, is my brother. I long for the brother I knew when the music of life was sweet.

In a recent devotional, Millie Snyder, executive paster of Myers Park Presbyterian Church, asked the question: "So, what does our faith say about suicide? Some claim it is an unforgivable sin, but we do not believe that to be true. A person in pain isn't condemned for wanting the pain to end. Suicide is tragic and leaves behind hurting people who will live with more questions than answers." I am that person with questions, and after all these years, I still need the answer to point me in a direction that somehow brings a return to the sweet music.

Snyder goes on to say, "People who feel hopeless or who want their pain to end need the faith community to be a place of safe welcome. The church can be that place if we are willing to acknowledge difficult topics and we are willing to listen to deep pain. God is with us and God offers hope through the love and care we are able to give to one another."[2]

Perhaps God is asking me to be part of that faith community, that place of safe welcome for those who feel hopeless. I never really knew my brother felt hopeless, and therein lies the simple truth and the pain. I should have known. Is it my guilt and my struggle with forgiving myself? Perhaps.

I do know that God was with Cal. He created him and loved him with a deep, forever love. If God can use me and help me grow up and get on with bringing hope and sweet music to others, then surely after finding the words for this book and tasting the few tears that my words gave, I will find relief, and blessed peace will follow.

TWENTY-TWO

Tears in Heaven

Tears are often the telescope by which men see far into heaven.

—Henry Ward Beecher

As you know by now, like my late grandmother Eunice Boone Crone and no telling how many other Scotch-Irish relatives, I am a weeper. After my sweet Grandmother Crone died, we had a lovely funeral for her, and the older adults assured me and the other grandkids that she was happily continuing to grow her violets and laugh out loud up in Heaven. But I was curious about whether she might still be shedding tears all the time like she did when she was sad, overjoyed, or as she said, "feeling sentimental." Then one day after I'd almost forgotten about it, I found the answer in the Bible when I learned that Jesus wept.

The words "Jesus wept," found in John 11:35 (the shortest verse in the Bible), are concise and to the point. John made it clear that Jesus was a man, a human, just like you and me, with the same feelings and struggles. His perfection was not diminished because He was a man. He was God's man, God's Son ... His Only Son! That was all I needed to convince me that, yes, there is a good chance we will cry in heaven.

C. H. Spurgeon, the great Victorian preacher, was one of the most influential people of the second half of the nineteenth century. In his celebrated 1865 sermon "No Tears in Heaven," Spurgeon shared about the time his mother told him that if he perished in hell, she would have to say "Amen" to his condemnation. He felt sure it was true, and although it sounded dreadful and succeeded in getting his attention, he thought, "Well, I love to think of your weeping over me far better than to think of you as a perfect being, with a tearless eye, looking on the damnation of your own child."[1] The thesis of his sermon was captured in his assertion:

"I do not believe that there will be one bit less tenderness, that there will be one fraction less of friendliness, and love, and sympathy—I believe there will be more—but that they will be in some way so refined and purified, that while compassion for suffering is there, hatred of sin will be there to balance it, and a state of complete equilibrium will be attained."[2]

In explaining how this will be achieved, Spurgeon suggested: "Perfect acceptance of the divine will is probably the secret of it; but it is not my business to guess; I don't know what handkerchief the Lord will use, but I do know that he will wipe away every tear from their eyes, and these tears are among them."[3]

The Bible tells us three times that God will wipe away all our tears. This promise first appears in the Old Testament: "He will swallow up death forever; and the Lord God will wipe away tears from all faces, and the reproach of his people he will take away from all the earth" (Isaiah 25:8 ESV). The second occurrence is found in the last book of the Bible: "For the Lamb in the midst of the throne will be their shepherd, and he will guide them to springs of living water, and God will wipe away every tear from their eyes" (Revelation 7:17 ESV). The final reference, also in Revelation, builds on this idea: "He will wipe away every tear from their eyes, and death shall be no more, neither shall there be mourning, nor crying, nor pain anymore, for the former things have passed away" (Revelation 21:4 ESV).

These words from the Bible make it clear that God *does* wipe away all tears. Though, in studying these verses, some Biblical scholars[4] have determined that this will happen after the Great White Throne Judgment foretold in Revelation and after the prophesied creation of the new heavens and the new earth: "For behold, I create new heavens and a new earth, and the former things shall not be remembered or come into mind" (Isaiah 65:17 ESV).

Will we shed tears in Heaven? Randy Alcorn believes we will through our divine connection with our LORD and through shared emotions. In his book *Heaven,* he gives a comprehensive look at what we should expect in heaven.[5] He points out that the Bible describes how people in Heaven have feelings—lots of good feelings. His vision of existence in Heaven includes expressing these feelings and emotions by enjoying our close relationship with God and with each other through laughing, eating, drinking, singing, playing, worshiping, and discovering a New Earth. Throughout Scripture, we learn that God has all kinds of emotions: anger, happiness, jealousy, and gladness. God takes delight in and rejoices over His people by expressing love, happiness, and laughter. Why would this ever come to an end in Heaven?

To be like God, made in His image, means to experience and to express the whole range of emotions, not just sadness. I agree with Alcorn and fully expect that this divine connection we humans have with our Creator may very well remain the same. I believe that in Heaven, if tears exist, they will continue to serve us and be messengers sent from our hearts for God's glory. Besides, I am a weeper and cannot imagine not having my tears in Heaven to express my feelings and know the fulfillment they bring. They are far from being just about sadness. They happen with all of our emotions and are there for us when words are not enough. Nonetheless, as Spurgeon says, the inexplicable answer to this question may be "perfect acceptance of divine will."[6]

I'll leave you with one important final thought about all of this guesswork, from William Barclay: "For the Christian, heaven is where Jesus is. We do not need to speculate on what heaven will be like. It is enough to know that we will be forever with him."[7]

TWENTY-THREE

Creatures That Capture Our Hearts

*Every good and perfect gift is from above, coming
down from the Father of the heavenly lights, who
does not change like shifting shadows.*
     —James 1:17

When I think about most of the people in my life, it's close
to impossible to come up with many friends, family
members, or neighbors who do not have pets, especially dogs,
who share their life and their love. These creatures are God's
gifts of joy and are part of the family, not separate entities or
just add-ons. In fact, much of family life revolves around our
pets. We spend time walking, feeding, and bathing them and
taking trips to the groomer and the vet. We search for pet sit-
ters of the highest caliber and character to care for our precious
pets when we are away—that is, if we cannot come up with any
possible way to take them with us. These pets are loved and
often are jokingly said to "run the show."

Humans are made in God's image with emotions and tears,
and we know that we have spiritual abilities that distinguish
us from other animals. We connect with God in worship and
prayer and we share a spiritual life with God who is a spirit.

Other creatures do not cry emotional tears, but do they have emotions?

Linda Simon, a licensed veterinarian, and veterinary consultant for the popular website ThePet.com, contends that dogs do not cry emotional tears, but they do experience a range of emotions including happiness, frustration, love, boredom, joy, grief, loyalty, and even sadness.[1] They may not cry to express emotions, but when you stop to consider how they show their love, hunger, need to go outside, or any other important message, you begin to get a picture that brings it all into focus. Dogs have distinctive ways of communicating needs and feelings. Like our babies, little puppies cry out for their mother. Whimpering and whining are the first ways that dogs learn to communicate. This continues throughout their lives, particularly if we respond with attention and affection. When dogs are anxious, even for happy reasons, they will often shake or tremble. Licking our faces (we like to think it's their way of kissing) and snuggling are familiar ways they show their feelings of love—ways that bring us joy. Just like humans, dogs use face and body language to communicate affection.

God has given us pets to be our incredible friends. In my family, we have all cried for each wonderful pet through the years. From guinea pigs and kittens to turtles, baby ducks, and, of course, our beloved dogs, emotional tears have been very much a part of making life complete when sharing it with our family creatures. We cried when the guinea pig got stuck in the wall for way too long before he was rescued, when our dog Domino was hit by a car, and, of course, when we said our last goodbyes at each animal's passing. These gifts from God have given us so much, and with their loving and forgiving ways, these animals have taught us so much. Our pets are such treasured examples and reminders of what God's devotion and goodness are all about.

A dear friend insists that her dog knows when she is sick or needs attention. He has a love language all his own. When he is snuggling, bringing her favorite little comfort pillow, and never leaving her side, my friend feels loved and has no doubt that the attention and love he lavishes on her during these times of need goes a long way to bring relief and wellness. Oscar Chavez, chief medical director of the website JustFoodForDogs.com, confirms that dogs are experts at reading human body language.[2] I have no doubt this is true. We have eight grandchildren and four "grand dogs." The grand dogs are extremely affectionate and loving with their families and with us when we come to visit. I've seen them "kiss" the tears right off the cheeks of my precious granddaughter's face as she recovered from an ugly bicycle accident. They can tell when any of their people are upset and come to the rescue like angels on a special mission.

With this much presence in our lives, and as deep as our emotions and feelings run for our animals, most of us have questions about their afterlife. Will we see them again in heaven? Do they have a spirit or soul that will live on? Humorist Will Rogers famously said, "If there are no dogs in heaven, then when I die, I want to go where they went."[3] This sure rings true because when we adore these special creatures, we have a hard time accepting that they will be gone, never again to lick our face, jump for joy when we enter the room, or snuggle next to us for comfort and good lovin'.

When it comes to answers about pets in heaven, Joni Eareckson Tada says it best: "If God brings our pets back to life, it wouldn't surprise me. It would be just like Him. It would be totally in keeping with His generous character … Heaven is going to be a place that will refract and reflect in as many ways as possible the goodness and joy of our great God, who delights in lavishing love on His children."[4]

When we read Isaiah 11:6–9, we get a glimpse into what heaven will be: a paradise where every animal could be a pet. They will all be tame, and fear will not separate us. Truly, God is perfection and we are His Beloved. So, in paradise, we know we will find absolute happiness and divine love. This will include music, dancing, each soul's favorite things, tears—sweet and happy tears of joy—and, surely, loving togetherness with animals. I like to think we'll be reunited with the ones with names we gave them, the ones we called our own.

TWENTY-FOUR

God's Extravagant Grace

"For I know the plans I have for you," declares the
LORD, "plans to prosper you and not to harm
you, plans to give you hope and a future."
—**Jeremiah 29:11**

Most all of us like the idea of princes and princesses. At some point, all little boys want to be a prince and all little girls want to find a prince. At the same time, all little girls want to be a princess and all little boys want to find a princess. I think it may very well be that throughout life, even at an early age, we are all searching for a happy ending and yearning to be a hero.

When we are young, most of us get to know our first princes in movies like *Snow White* and *Cinderella*. They are all dashingly handsome, very brave, and gallant. They do all the right things to win the battle, sweep a girl off her feet, and save the day. Then there are the other male heroes like Robin Hood, Zorro, Batman, Superman, Harry Potter, and my grandson's favorites, which are all the princes of the Pokémon universe. And what about the princesses who went from ordinary to spectacular, like Snow White and Cinderella? I should also not neglect mentioning the fabulous female superheroes like Wonder Woman, Catwoman, Storm, and Anna and Elsa, both of my granddaughters' favorites, from the movie *Frozen*.

I have shared with you the ups and downs of my love life, and you might be thinking that it was all rather sad with my relationships ending badly. I can almost hear my granddaughter saying, "Where are the happy parts?" I love happy endings, too. So, I decided to end this book with the story of my prince.

After leaving my children, their father, and our home behind in South Carolina, I moved to Charlotte physically, while my spirit and those things I treasured most were far enough away to make it difficult to adjust. I enjoyed what I still call the best job of my life, nice new friends at work, and a condo in one of the best parts of Charlotte, but I spent most of my personal time either travelling back and forth to Spartanburg, as I mentioned earlier, or making sure my boys were with me whenever possible. This worked for most of the first year. I stayed busy and settled into my routine.

Eventually, since I was legally divorced, I decided that it was okay to date, even though I did not want to ever get married again. I did not want to meet anyone I even halfway liked, as I was content to just work, go to the gym, and find time to be with my kids whenever possible. Besides, it was an unusual experience to suddenly become a "single chick" again. There actually should be classes on how to do that; I sure could have used the help.

My first real dates involved awkward moments of not knowing what to say, how to act, or even what to wear. There were no dating services or websites back in those days, and for a new girl in town, there were few options for meeting people—any people, not just men. Admittedly, I did not try hard, and I actually did not care that much. I focused on my work and figured my new life would just have to take care of itself.

Then, out of the blue, when I least expected it (as they say), a new friend asked me if I might be interested in meeting one of her neighbors who had recently divorced. She said we had lots in common (snow-skiing and a love of sports), and that, like me, he was not looking for a serious relationship. Plus, he was a nice guy.

If I had been watching a movie, at that point I would have rolled my eyes and said, "Sure, he's a nice guy—this is for sure going to be a disaster!" What were the chances that a 50-year-old woman would meet the right 50-year-old man during the first year of her "suddenly single" older person's life? Whatever the chances, it happened. We met, we liked each other, and we did have plenty in common. Best of all, my precious boys liked him too.

Yes, after all the years of trying to control everything, I had surrendered this to God and humbly backed off. I prayed often to the finest prince of all—The Prince of Peace.[1] I cried often and, as before, I had a few glasses of wine and smoked a few cigarettes to take on the general aura of a lonely single woman. What made the difference? God's grace—His extravagant grace. I did nothing to deserve it; I didn't even know that I wanted a difference. But the truth—the amazing, mysterious truth— was that I am God's Beloved and He had plans for me.

I had been ashamed and heartbroken and was struggling to make a new life. I had been totally turned off to the idea of ever getting emotionally involved with any other man. Why would I?

I was a failure at relationships and had never been able to make one really work. But neither had he, although you would never have known it. Vance was handsome and seemed confident and well-adjusted, but he had the same struggles and much the same track record as I did. God had plans for him too.

The rest is, without a doubt, a story made in heaven. I know that sounds corny, but it's true. We dated, happily most of the time, for five years, but never planned to get married. And yet. That's right! Despite all of our trying to control our lives, all of our weaknesses and mistakes, we found each other and it just would not do to turn the other way. I found my prince when I was not even looking for him. He found me—his princess. I love writing that he found his princess but blush as I see it on the screen. Am I really a princess? Is he really a prince? I am not sure, but Vance and I have been married twenty-three years now. I will let you decide.

One thing I am sure of from the bottom of my heart, through every tear I've ever cried, is this: I am God's beloved— and so are you!

We will all have happy endings when we surrender them to God. He has plans for each of us, plans that are custom-made and delivered with His extravagant grace. Throughout this book I have shared with you how I searched for what I would be someday. I found my answer and it is your answer as well. You will always be: LOVED!

Thank you for sharing this closing corny story with me. I wish you inner beauty, your own corny stories, and true knowing with your every tear, your every breath, and with every blink of your eyes that You Are His Beloved and forever will be!

Acknowledgments

To my precious sister Jimmie Janice Miller, who supported me in publishing this little book, then reviewed each chapter and gave me ideas that expanded my thoughts and brought new words. Her caring support made being a nonfiction author a wonderful adventure.

To my community of prayer partners. You know who you are. Please realize how much I love you and cherish each of my sweet angels here on earth.

To my editor Kathy Brown who not only took my words and made them sing, but who patiently walked me through every step of making my vision come to life. She was there each time I needed her with professional advice and assistance as well as a warm and loving heart.

To Maureen Ryan Griffin, my coach and mentor, who welcomed me in the beginning with my ideas, my pages and pages of notes, and with an open mind and a wide-open heart. Her support and nudging to "make it more personal" took me from academic writing with my head to nonfiction spiritual writing from my heart.

To Adam Thomas whose designs gave life to my visions and my words. Thank you for sharing your many talents and your love of our LORD that shown through as we created together.

And above all, to my family: husband Vance, children Jimmy and Jeff, stepchildren Brian and Catherine, and all eight grandchildren in alphabetical order: Andrew, Carlee, Devin, Griffin, Luke, Noah, Reed, and Stella. You are my life.

About the Author

Diann Cockerham, EdD, is a consultant and career counselor who went from secretary to cum laude BBA graduate and on to winning national awards selling medical products and serving ten years in healthcare management. Then everything changed. With God's loving help, she adjusted, and went on to spend twelve years as a successful college administrator guiding hundreds of college students in finding their career path. She is a nonfiction author, a skier who dreams of living in the Colorado Rockies, a weeper, and an expert on emotions who thrives on helping others find their unique, God-ordained path through life and all the changes along the way. She enjoys speaking and writing about her study of college students' emotions as well as sharing her perspective on the spirituality of emotions. She is a native Tennessean who now lives in Charlotte, North Carolina, with her husband. Their family of four adult children and eight grandchildren is their everything.

A Note from Diann

Word-of-mouth is essential for any author to succeed. If you enjoyed *Exquisite Tears*, please leave a review online – anywhere you are able. Even just a sentence or two would make all the difference and would be very much appreciated.

With gratitude,

Diann

Endnotes

Introduction

1   Diann Cockerham, "Exploring Students' Emotional Experience Within the Distance Learning Environment" (doctoral dissertation, Argosy University, 2011).

2   Mark Batterson, *Whisper: How to Hear the Voice of God* (New York: Multnomah, 2017), 86.

Chapter 1: Crying is Good for You

1   Judith Orloff, "The Health Benefits of Tears," *HuffPost*, last modified November 17, 2011, https://www.huffpost.com/entry/emotional-wellness_b_653754.

2   William Frey, *Crying: The Mystery of Tears* (New York: Winston Press, 1985).

3   Orloff, "The Health Benefits of Tears."

4   Ad Vingerhoets, "Why Do Only Humans Cry?" *Ad Vingerhoets*, last modified 2014, http://www.advingerhoets.com/.

Chapter 2: Salt of the Earth

1   "Why Is the Ocean Salty, But Rivers Flowing into it are Not?" *National Ocean Service*, February 26, 2021, https://oceanservice.noaa.gov/facts/riversnotsalty.html.

2   Ibid.

3   "What Does Salt of the Earth Mean?" *Bible Study*, accessed April 12, 2021, https://biblestudy.org/question/salt-of-the-earth.html.

4   Billy Graham, "Answers by Billy Graham," *Billy Graham Evangelistic Association*, last modified May 16, 2008, https://billygraham.org/answer/what-will-we-look-like-when-we-get-to-heaven-will-we-just-be-spirits-or-something-like-that-floating-around-from-place-to-place-but-not-being-anything-solid/.

5   Diann Cockerham, "A Sacred Pinch of Salt," *Exquisite Tears*, 2021.

Chapter 3: God Collects Our Tears

1   "Tear Bottle History," *Lachrymatory.com*, last modified May 22, 2008, www.lachrymatory.com/History.htm.

2   Vingerhoets, "Why Do Only Humans Cry?"

3   Frank DeLaney, *Ireland: A Novel* (New York: Harper, 2008).

4   "About Tear Bottles," *Perfect Memorials*, accessed April 15, 2021, https://www.perfectmemorials.com/tear-bottles-c- 919.html.

Chapter 4: Love and Tears: A Powerful Combination

1   "Why God Gave Women Tears," *Parish of St. Ignatius*, May 12, 2019, http://www.stignatiustoowong.org.au/newsletterar-chive/2019/0512.pdf.

Chapter 5: Why Men Cry

1   Derek Whitney, "Why Is It So Hard for Me to Cry?" *PsychCentral* (blog), *Healthline Media*, October 12, 2012, https://psychcentral.com/blog/why-is-it-so-hard-for-men-to-cry#1.

2   "Beowoulf," *The Project Gutenberg eBook of Beowulf*, last modi-fied July 19, 2005, https://www.gutenberg.org/files/16328/16328-h/16328-h.htm.

3   Whitney, "Why Is It So Hard for Me to Cry?"

4   Tom Lutz, *Crying: The Natural and Cultural History of Tears* (New York: Norton, 2001).

5   Daphne Rose Kingma, *The Men We Never Knew: How to Deepen Your Relationship with the Man You Love* (San Francisco: Conari Press, 1994).

6   Barbara Markway, "How to Crack the Code of Men's Feelings," *Psychology Today*, January 18, 2014, https://www.psychologytoday.com/us/blog/living-the-questions/201401/how-crack-the-code-men-s-feelings.

7   Théoden Janes, "Did Luke Kuechly Make it Safe for a Man to Cry?" *Charlotte Observer*, November 19, 2016.

8   Ibid.

9   Emma Watson, "Emma Watson: Gender Equality Is Your Issue Too," *UNWomen,* September 20, 2014, https://www.unwomen.org/en/news/stories/2014/9/emma-watson-gender-equality-is-your-is-sue-too.

Chapter 6: Emotional Intelligence

1   Joyce J. Endendijk et al. "Gender-Differentiated Parenting Revisited: Meta-Analysis Reveals Very Few Differences in Parental Control of Boys and Girls," *National Library of Medicine, PubMed.gov*, July 15, 2016, https://doi.org/10.1371/journal.pone.0159193.

2   Dolores Smyth, "5 Ways to Teach Your Children That Emotions Are Important," *Crosswalk*, May 30, 2019, https://www.crosswalk.com/

family/parenting/kids/ways-to-teach-your-children-that-emotions-are-important.html.

3   *The Cambridge Dictionary, Online Edition,* (Cambridge: Cambridge University Press, 2021), s.v. "Emotional Intelligence," accessed April 12, 2021, https://dictionary.cambridge.org/us/dictionary/english/emotional-intelligence.

4   Daniel Goleman, *Emotional Intelligence* (New York: Bantam Dell, 1995).

5   Susan Humphrey-Murto et al. "Does Emotional Intelligence at Medical School Admission Predict Future Academic Performance?" *Academic Medicine Journal of AAMC,* 89, no. 4 (April 2014), doi: 10.1097/ACM.0000000000000165.

6   Sharon A. Gutman et al. "Emotional Intelligence Admission Essay Scale: Comparison Between Interview and Essay Formats," *Annals of International Occupational Therapy,* 2, no. 1 (April 17, 2018), https://doi.org/10.3928/24761222-20180417-02.

7   Robert Kellemen, "Emotions: What Does the Bible Teach?" *RPM Ministries,* March 25, 2014, https://rpmministries.org/2014/03/emotions-what-does-the-bible-teach/.

Chapter 7: Is Crying a Sign of Weakness?

1   Brett and Kate McKay, "The 15 Greatest Man Cries (Plus 5 Dishonorable Mentions)," *Art of Manliness,* last modified September 28, 2020, https://www.artofmanliness.com/articles/15-great-men-that-cried/.

2   Andrew Roberts, "Winston Wept: The Extraordinary Lachrymosity and Romantic Imagination of Winston Churchill," *International Churchill Society,* Autumn 2016, https://winstonchurchill.org/publications/finest-hour/finest-hour- 174/winston-wept/.

3   McKay, "The 15 Greatest Man Cries."

4   Ibid.

5   "The Queen Does Cry, Even If 'The Crown' Makes You Think Otherwise," *Marie Claire,* November 18, 2019, https://www.marieclaire.com/celebrity/a29523273/queen-elizabeth-crying-photos-the-crown/.

6   Charles Dickens, *The Old Curiosity Shop* (London: Penguin, Ltd., 1841).

7   *Collins English Dictionary, Complete and Unabridged,* 12th ed. (Glasgow: Harper Collins, 2014), s.v. "Weaker Sex," accessed April 29, 2021, https://www.thefreedictionary.com/weaker+sex.

8   Vingerhoets, "Why Do Only Humans Cry?"

9   Gary Brown, "The Wisdom of Crying," *Dr. Gary Brown*, June 26, 2018, https://drgarybrowntherapy.com/wisdom-of-crying/.

10 "Affliction … Prepares an Ordinary Person for … An Extraordinary Destiny," *The Wisdom of C. S. Lewis,* August 27, 2011, blog, https://cslewiswisdom.blogspot.com/2011/08/afflictionprepares-ordinary-person.html.

Chapter 8: The Beauty of Tears

1   Victoria Moran, *Lit from Within* (New York: Harper Collins, 2001), 244.

2   Moran, *Lit from Within*.

Chapter 9: Being True to Yourself

1   Wayne Dyer, "The Power of I Am," *Dr. Wayne W. Dyer*, accessed March 31, 2021, https://www.drwaynedyer.com/blog/the-power-of-i-am/.

Chapter 10: Repentant Tears

1   Horace Mann, "Horace Mann Quotes," https://www.goodreads.com/author/quotes/279932.Horace_Mann.

2   Thomas Dixon, "Tracks of My Tears: The Mystery of Crying," ABC Radio transcript, July 21, 2013, https://www.abc.net.au/radionational/programs/archived/bodysphere/tracks-of-my-tears3a-the-mystery-of-crying/4821348#transcript.

3   Dr. Bryce Klabunde, "'I'll Change, I Promise'—Six Signs of Genuine Repentance," *Mark W. Gaither*, June 2, 2009, https://markwgaither.com/2009/06/02/ill-change-i-promise-six-signs-of-genuine-repentance/.

Chapter 11: No Two Tears Are Alike

1   Lettie Cowman, *Streams in the Desert* (Grand Rapids: Zondervan Corporation, 1997).

2   "Is It True That No Two Snow Crystals Are Alike?" *Everyday Mysteries, Library of Congress*, November 19, 2019, https://www.loc.gov/everyday-mysteries/meteorology-climatology/item/is-it-true-that-no-two-snow-crystals-are-alike/.

3   Kiri Picone, "7 Totally Awesome (and Terrifying) Objects Under a Microscope," *All That's Interesting,* January 12, 2018, https://allthatsinteresting.com/objects-under-a-microscope.

4   Rose-Lynn Fisher, *The Topography of Tears* (New York: Bellevue Literary Press, 2017).

5   Fisher, *The Topography of Tears.*

Chapter 12: Tears and The Green-Eyed Monster

1   Erica Cirino, "How Our Eyes Grow and Change as We Get Older," *Healthline*, last modified October 21, 2019, https://www.healthline. com/health/do-your-eyes-grow.

2   Sara Lindberg, "When Do Babies' Eyes Change Color?", *Healthline Parenthood*, last modified June 10, 2020, https://www.healthline. com/health/baby/when-do-babies-eyes-change-color#melanin.

3   Nancy Moyer, "Eye Spy: Worldwide Eye Color Percentages," *Healthline,* last modified November 21, 2019, https://www.healthline.com/ health/eye-health/eye-color-percentages.

4   *Merriam-Webster Dictionary, Online Edition,* (Springfield: Merriam-Webster, Inc., 2021), s.v. "Jealous vs. Envious," accessed March 17, 2021, https://www.merriam-webster.com/words-at-play/jealous-vs-envious.

5   Glennon Doyle (formerly Glennon Doyle Melton), "How to Train Your Monsters," *I Have a Forever* (reblog), February 16, 2015, https://ihaveaforever.wordpress.com/tag/glennon-doyle-melton/.

6   Henry Nouwen, *You Are the Beloved* (New York: Convergent, 2017).

Chapter 13: Laughing and Crying

1   Kahlil Gibran, "On Joy and Sorrow," *Poets*, accessed May 25, 2021, https://poets.org/poem/joy-and-sorrow.

2   Jan Karon, *To Be Where You Are* (New York: G.P. Putnam's Sons, 2017).

3   Amanda Casanova, "What Causes Those Happy Tears at the Finish Line," *Women's Running*, February 21, 2018, https://www.womensrunning.com/culture/happy-tears-crying-finish-line/.

4   Mike Downie, "Laughing and Crying is the Soundtrack of our Lives," *The Nature of Things*, produced by CBC, podcast, accessed March 27, 2021, https://www.cbc.ca/natureofthings/blog/laughing-and-crying-is-the-soundtrack-of-our-lives.

Chapter 14: Tears of Deep Gratitude

1   Andy Otto, "Why Grace is Revealed in Gratitude," *The Georgia Bulletin*, November 13, 2020, https://georgiabulletin.org/commentary/2020/11/why-grace-is-revealed-in-gratitude/.

2   Otto, "Why Grace is Revealed in Gratitude."

3   Thornton Wilder, *The Woman of Andros* (Greenwich Village: Boni & Liveright, 1930).

4   Sri Chinmoy, *God Is…: Selected Writings of Sri Chinmoy* (Haldwani: Aum Pubns, 1997).

Chapter 15: Forgiving Yourself with Tears

1   C. S. Lewis, *The Collected Letters of C. S. Lewis* (San Francisco: Harper, 2005).

Chapter 17: Imagination: Clowns, Dolls, and Grown-up Tears

1   Norman Vincent Peale, *Positive Imaging: The Powerful Way to Change Your Life* (New York: Open Road Media, 2015).

2   Helen Keller, *The World I Live in and Optimism: A Collection of Essays* (New York: Dover Publications; 2010).

Chapter 18: Creativity and Emotions

1   Daniel Wallen, "9 Surprising Benefits of Crying, or Why It's Okay to Have a Good Cry," *Lifehack*, accessed November 13, 2020, https://www.lifehack.org/articles/lifestyle/9-surprising-benefits-crying-why-its-okay-have-good-cry.html.

2   Wallen, "9 Surprising Benefits of Crying."

3   Robert Frost, "The Figure a Poem Makes," *Collected Poems of Robert Frost* (New York: Holt, Rinehart, and Winston, 1939).

4   *Pretty Woman*, directed by Garry Marshall (1990; Beverly Hills, CA: Touchstone Pictures), Film.

5   Robertson, "Do Schools Kill Creativity?" February 2006, TED video, https://www.ted.com/talks/sir_ken_robinson_do_schools_kill_creativity.

6   Scott Barry Kaufman, "The Emotions That Make Us More Creative," *Harvard Business Review*, August 12, 2015, https://hbr.org/2015/08/the-emotions-that-make-us-more-creative.

7   Jessica Chastain, "Jessica Chastain and Being a Highly Sensitive Person," *Highly Sensitive*, accessed November 14, 2021, https://highlysensitive.org/602/jessica-chastain-and-high-sensitivity/.

8   Jamie Anderson, *Taylor Swift: The Ultimate Taylor Swift Fan Book 2020* (Melbourne: Bellanova Books, 2019).

9   Robertson, "Do Schools Kill Creativity?"

10 Sophia Loren, *Women & Beauty* (London: Aurum Press, 1984).

Chapter 19: Achieving Balance

1   William Arthur Ward, *Rewarding Moments: A Treasure of Prose and Poetry* (Coshocton, Ohio: Shaw-Barton, Inc., 1st ed., 1989), 118.

2   Trevor Hudson, *The Serenity Prayer: A Simple Prayer to Enrich Your Life* (Nashville: Upper Room Books, 2012), 89. (Biblical quotes included by Hudson.)

3   Trey Gowdy, *Doesn't Hurt to Ask: Using the Power of Questions to Communicate, Connect, and Persuade* (New York: Crown Forum, 2020).

4   Gowdy, *Doesn't Hurt to Ask.*

5   Ibid.

6   Ibid.

7   Ish N. Mishra, "Plato's Theory of Soul," *Countercurrents*, August 10, 2018, https://countercurrents.org/2018/08/platos-theory-of-soul/.

8   "Do We Have Both a Soul and a Spirit?" *Answers, Billy Graham Evangelistic Association*, last modified June 1, 2004, https://billygraham.org/answer/do-we-have-both-a-soul-and-a-spirit/.

9   Witness Lee, "Dealing with Our Inward Parts for the Growth in Life," *Living Stream Ministry*, accessed February 4, 2021, https://www.ministrysamples.org/excerpts/THE-SOUL-HAVING-THREE-PARTS.HTML.

10 Deuteronomy 6:5, 26:16; Matthew 22:37; Mark 12:30; Mark 12:33.

11 Lee, "Dealing with Our Inward Parts for the Growth in Life."

Chapter 20: Hugs, Kisses, or Tears

1   Charles Finch, *The Vanishing Man* (New York: Minotaur Books, 2019), 270.

2   Robert Mcg. Thomas Jr., "Leo Buscaglia, TV Advocate of Love's Power, Dies at 74," *The New York Times*, June 13, 1998, https://www.nytimes.com/1998/06/13/arts/leo-buscaglia-tv-advocate-of-love-s-power-dies-at-74.html.

3   *Three Little Words*, directed by Richard Thorpe (1950; Burbank, CA: Warner Bros.), Film.

4   Karyn Hall, *The Emotionally Sensitive Person* (Oakland: New Harbinger Publications, 2014).

5   Hall, *The Emotionally Sensitive Person.*

6   C. S. Lewis, *Letters to Malcolm: Chiefly on Prayer,* (Buena Vista: Mariner Books, 1st ed., November 4, 2002), *Goodreads,* accessed November 15, 2020.

Chapter 21: When the Crying Stops

1 Louisa May Alcott, *Little Women* (Boston: Roberts Brothers, 1868).
2 Millie Snyder, Daily Devotional from Myers Park Presbyterian Church, July 29, 2018.

Chapter 22: Tears in Heaven

1 C. H. Spurgeon, *No Tears in Heaven*, accessed November 15, 2020, https://www.spurgeongems.org/sermon/chs643.pdf.
2 Spurgeon, *No Tears in Heaven*.
3 Ibid.
4 Jim Butcher, "Why There Are Tears in Heaven," *Sermon Central*, last modified November 22, 2004, https://www.sermoncentral.com/sermons/why-there-are-tears-in-heaven-jim-butcher-sermon-on-heaven-74073.
5 Randy Alcorn, *Heaven* (Carol Stream: Tyndale Momentum, 2011).
6 Spurgeon, *No Tears in Heaven*.
7 "Collected Quotes of William Barclay," *Tentmaker*, accessed June 13, 2021, https://www.tentmaker.org/biographies/barclayquotes.htm.

Chapter 23: Creatures That Capture Our Hearts

1 Charlotte Hilton Andersen, "Do Dogs Cry?" *Reader's Digest*, December 30, 2020, https://www.rd.com/article/do-dogs-cry/.
2 Charlotte Hilton Anderson, "28 Ways Your Pet is Trying to Say I Love You," *Reader's Digest*, December 3, 2019, https://www.rd.com/list/ways-pet-says-i-love-you/.
3 Bryan Sterling, *Will Rogers Speaks: Over 1000 Timeless Quotations for Public Speakers,* (Lanham: M. Evans & Company, 1995).
4 Joni Eareckson Tada, *Heaven: What Will it Be Like?* (United Kingdom: Marshall Pickering, 1999).

Chapter 24: God's Extravagant Grace

1 Isaiah 9:6